Strategic Conspiracy Narratives

Strategic Conspiracy Narratives proposes an innovative semiotic perspective for analysing how contemporary conspiracy theories are used for shaping interpretation paths and identities of a targeted audience.

Conspiracy theories play a significant role in the viral spread of misinformation that has an impact on the formation of public opinion about certain topics. They allow the connecting of different events that have taken place in various times and places and involve several actors that seem incompatible to bystanders. This book focuses on strategic-function conspiracy narratives in the context of (social) media and information conflict. It explicates the strategic devices in how conspiracy theories can be used to evoke a hermeneutics of suspicion – a permanent scepticism and questioning of so-called mainstream media channels and dominant public authorities, delegitimisation of political opponents, and the ongoing search for hidden clues and coverups. The success of strategic dissemination of conspiracy narratives depends on the cultural context, specifics of the targeted audience and the semiotic construction of the message. This book proposes an innovative semiotic perspective for analysing contemporary strategic communication. The authors develop a theoretical framework that is based on the semiotics of culture, the notions of strategic narrative and transmedia storytelling.

This book is targeted to specialists and graduate students working on social theory, semiotics, journalism, strategic communication, social media and contemporary social problems in general.

Mari-Liis Madisson received her PhD in Semiotics and Culture Studies from the University of Tartu, Estonia in 2016. She is a Research Fellow at the Department of Semiotics at the University of Tartu and a visiting Research Fellow at School of History, Anthropology, Philosophy and Politics at the Queen´s University Belfast, UK. Her research combines cultural semiotics, political semiotics, communication and media studies. Her research interests lie in online culture, conspiracy theories, information influence activities and extreme right communication. She is the author of *The Semiotic Construction of Identities in Hypermedia Environments: The Analysis of Online Communication of the Estonian Extreme Right* (2016).

Andreas Ventsel is a senior researcher of semiotics at Tartu University, Estonia. He holds an MA degree and a PhD in Semiotics. He teaches a range of subjects in semiotics, society and politics, cultural theory, and research seminars. His research is interdisciplinary, which includes semiotics, discourse theory, visual communication, rhetoric and political analysis with particular focus on post-structural political thought. Since 2007, Ventsel has participated in several research projects in the fields of semiotics, visual studies and strategic communication. He has presented the results of research on these topics in around 100 academic articles and has been the editor of several Estonian-based and international scientific journals. He is the author of *Towards Semiotic Theory of Hegemony* (2009).

Conspiracy Theories
Series Editors: Peter Knight, *University of Manchester*,
and **Michael Butter**, *University of Tübingen.*

Conspiracy theories have a long history and exist in all modern societies. However, their visibility and significance are increasing today. Conspiracy theories can no longer be simply dismissed as the product of a pathological mindset located on the political margins.

This series provides a nuanced and scholarly approach to this most contentious of subjects. It draws on a range of disciplinary perspectives including political science, sociology, history, media and cultural studies, area studies and behavioural sciences. Issues covered include the psychology of conspiracy theories, changes in conspiratorial thinking over time, the role of the Internet, regional and political variations, and the social and political impact of conspiracy theories.

The series will include edited collections, single-authored monographs and short-form books.

The Stigmatization of Conspiracy Theory since the 1950s
"A Plot to Make us Look Foolish"
Katharina Thalmann

Conspiracy Theories in Turkey
Conspiracy Nation
Doğan Gürpınar

Routledge Handbook of Conspiracy Theories
Edited by Michael Butter and Peter Knight

Contemporary Conspiracy Culture
Truth and Knowledge in an Era of Epistemic Instability
Jaron Harambam

Strategic Conspiracy Narratives
A Semiotic Approach
Mari-Liis Madisson and Andreas Ventsel

Strategic Conspiracy Narratives

A Semiotic Approach

**Mari-Liis Madisson and
Andreas Ventsel**

Routledge
Taylor & Francis Group

LONDON AND NEW YORK

First published 2021
by Routledge
2 Park Square, Milton Park, Abingdon, Oxon OX14 4RN

and by Routledge
52 Vanderbilt Avenue, New York, NY 10017

Routledge is an imprint of the Taylor & Francis Group, an informa business

British Library Cataloguing-in-Publication Data
A catalogue record for this book is available from the British Library

Library of Congress Cataloging-in-Publication Data
Names: Madisson, Mari-Liis, 1988 – author. | Ventsel, Andreas,
1976 – author.
Title: Strategic conspiracy narratives: a semiotic approach/Mari-Liis
Madisson and Andreas Ventsel.
Description: Milton Park, Abingdon, Oxon; New York, NY: Routledge,
2020. |
Series: Conspiracy theories | Includes bibliographical references and
index.
Identifiers: LCCN 2020001487 (print) | LCCN 2020001488 (ebook)
Subjects: LCSH: Conspiracy theories. | Soros, George.
Classification: LCC HV6275.M33 2020 (print) | LCC HV6275 (ebook) |
DDC 001.9-dc23
LC record available at https://lccn.loc.gov/2020001487
LC ebook record available at https://lccn.loc.gov/2020001488

ISBN: 978-0-367-03098-8 (hbk)
ISBN: 978-0-429-02038-4 (ebk)

Typeset in Times New Roman
by Wearset Ltd, Boldon, Tyne and Wear

Contents

Acknowledgements

We would like to express our sincere gratitude to all who have contributed into developing our ideas on conspiracy theories and publishing this book.

Special thanks go to all members of COST 15101 and especially Michael Butter and Peter Knight for leading this inspiring and thought-provoking project. Many thanks also to our comrades from the East-European picnic club: Anastasiya Astapova, Onoriu Colăcel, Corneliu Pintilescu, Ivan Brlić, Franciszek Czech, and its French and Swedish "correspondence members" Julien Giry and Andreas Önnerfors for their support and friendship which made all our conferences unforgettable events.

We are indebted to many of our colleagues from Tartu University who have supported and inspired our academic endeavours in several ways. We would especially like to thank Lauri Linask for his insightful feedback to the draft of our manuscript and Ene-Reet Soovik for translating our book into English.

This work was supported by the research grants PRG314 "Semiotic fitting as a mechanism of biocultural diversity: instability and sustainability in novel environments", PUTJD804 "Semiotic perspective on the analysis of strategic conspiracy narratives" and SHVFI19127 "Strategic Narrative as a Model for Reshaping the Security Dilemma".

Last, but not least thanks go to our cat Werner – the greatest and most powerful conspirator and an endless source of inspiration.

Introduction

Especially after Donald Trump's presidential campaign and the Brexit referendum in 2016, the power of viral conspiracy theories related with disinformation and misinformation crusades has become undeniable. In strategic communication, conspiracy theories have proved themselves as an effective means of creating distrust or even fear of and disdain towards political opponents, of spicing up points being made and constructing a positive self-image of moral superiority. Even if we consider ourselves as media literate citizens capable of critical thinking, we may have met catchy explanations that link certain social events and real persons with intriguing conspiracy references. For instance, we may have heard that there is no human-induced climate crisis, and that the Swedish environmental activist Greta Thunberg is a puppet of a globalist influence network; that Hillary Clinton is linked to a secret cabal of paedophiles and Satanists; that the 2016 European migration crisis or Coronavirus (COVID-19) was actually launched by George Soros and his minions as part of their plan to destroy nation states and control the population. Conspiracy theories serve as successful attention grabbers, as they link topical events with forceful and fairly easily graspable meanings and, as a rule, also contain a fair share of mystery and thrills – after all, they talk of the insidious deeds of a sinister group that have remained hidden from the public despite all anti-corruption means taken and instances of surveillance involved. Conspiracy theories are well-suited to a sharing culture based on quick reactions and the rather limited argumentation of social media which provides simple, funny and intriguing explanations an opportunity to become viral and to stick.

Under the conditions of contemporary information overload, conspiracy theories are valued highly as they function as features that make it possible to draw meaningful connected images from the jumble of dots that bits and pieces of information consist of. What is more, they often offer ready-made templates, on the basis of which members of so-called "enlightened audiences" can draw similar connecting lines in future interpreting situations and thus find proof to the existence of conspiracies in random data. A conspiracy theory can function as an important anchor point of the interpretation process and is thus potentially much more dangerous than discrete false statements or fake news, as it often directs the audience towards interpretations of whole series of events that have actually taken place, as well as various facts, in their own hyper sceptical light (Benkler et al. 2018, 34). It is important to emphasise that although fake news that has been produced with the aim of deliberately disinforming the audience may also be a conspiracy theory, no sign of equation can be put between them, for conspiracy theories represent a certain type of meaning relations that fake news need not necessarily involve. Namely, conspiracy theories outline a specific narrative explanation that sees "a group of people acting in secret to nefarious end" (Birchall 2006, 34) as the driving force behind events. In contrast to fake news, contemporary conspiracy theories are not created only because of someone's wish to disinform the target wittingly, as their authors may also articulate such theories for their sincere fear of conspiracies or due to a playful wish to explain some occurrence via a conspiracy.

The main goal of our book is to study the function of conspiracy theories in various contemporary information conflicts and influencing activities – we are interested in how, on the one hand, conspiracy theories can be applied as a tool in attention grabbing and targeting of audiences, and how they can be used to generate alienation; and, on the other hand, how they are used to construct positive self-images and moral victim positions. Despite the topicality and relevance of this research focus, no systematic studies have been published as of yet that concentrate on strategic conspiracy theories in relation with the information influencing activities occurring in contemporary digital media.

Determining the theoretical framework

Many of us are familiar with Umberto Eco's famous sentence "Semiotics is in principle the discipline studying everything which can be used in order to lie" (Eco 1976, 7). Eco adds: "If something cannot be used to tell a lie, conversely it cannot be used to tell the truth: it cannot in fact be used 'to tell' at all" (ibid.). Indeed, the essential conventionality of sign processes, as well as the acceptance of the possibility of lying or being mistaken in meaning-making, is a part of the foundational principles of the semiotic approach, and the analysis of the success or failure of communication has been taken as one of the main tasks of semiotics as a discipline. This is one of the reasons why we believe that a semiotic approach is innovative for/in describing and conceptualising conspiracy theories circulating on social networking sites (SNSs), because it makes it possible to understand multimodal and intertextual combinations of various texts and different patterns of interaction co-evolving with those texts (see Leone et al. 2020).

This book has a predominantly theoretical focus and its main theoretical body relies on the concept of *strategic narrative* developed in the tradition politics of international relations, work in the field of cultural semiotics and existing semiotic studies of conspiracy theories. These conceptual frameworks are developed further by taking into account the specifics of social media communication. Our aim is to elaborate a theoretical-analytical framework meant for analysing conspiracy theories in the context of strategic communication, and we will illustrate our conceptual framework with several examples of theories related to George Soros that demonstrate various angles of strategic meaning-making.

Before we proceed to a brief introduction of the book's contents, we explain the selection principles of the theoretical framework we aim to create and define its field of application. We consider *strategic communication* as an umbrella term that covers various long-term and goal-oriented communication activities, such as *strategic planning, media development, audience design, image care*, etc. In its broadest meaning it is "purposeful use of communication by an organisation to fulfil its mission" (Hallahan et al. 2007, 3). Generally speaking, strategic communication management has to balance three factors: the message(s), the media channel(s) and the audience(s) (Bockstette 2008). The present book first and foremost focuses on the level of the message, as our main aim is to create an analytical frame with the help of which to study meaning-making in strategic conspiracy narratives and how this meaning making shapes the target audience. We regard meaning-making as a process through which participants in communication attempt to understand each other and the world, to influence their conversation partners and, in some cases, even mislead them.

We are aware of the difficulties that researchers meet when facing the discussion of the multidirectional and asymmetric meaning-making in social media. For instance, questions of the goal-oriented and intentionality of text creation arise in studying strategic communication: to what degree is it possible to determine the real authors of texts and their original aims in the hybrid information stream of social media; whether and to what extent can an organisation or an actor be attributed concrete communicative aims. We find that in combining the notions of the strategic narrative currently gaining popularity in the discipline of international relations, and Umberto Eco's concepts of the Model Reader and the Model Author as the frameworks for text creation strategies, we will be able to offer an original treatment focusing on meaning-making processes and provide these questions with answers in the context of strategic conspiracy narratives. Our model first and foremost emphasises the unity of the strategic devices which is primarily constructed on the level of the text.

In connection with this question, it is important to discover whether, and to what degree, the information stream of (social) media and particular posts as information fragments that often have a limited linear textual component, can be considered as narrative. According to Eco (2005, 77–78), non-narrative texts can be expanded and made narrative for the purpose of analysis if the possibilities the texts include are actualised. As researchers, we can construct the narrative unity on the more abstract level of the analysis of the text corpus – the event of conflict, the characters participating in it, the context surrounding the event etc., even though all the formal characteristics of narrative do not appear explicitly in a particular text.

We also feel compelled to specify some things in connection with the ontology of our research object. Our main focus of attention is directed at semiotic analysis of the textual strategies of conspiracy narratives circulating in online environments; so we will study in more depth particular textual units (e.g. videos, social media posts, news items, blog entries, etc.) that mediate conspiracy theories and the socio-communicative context of their spreading. Thus, in the framework of this study we shall not explore macro-sociological factors concerning, e.g. power relations that depend on the infrastructure of social media and the accessibility of big data, nor digital divides existing within the population, etc.

Neither do we study the relationship of the identities shaped on social media with other (also offline) identity-creating practices of the subjects. We proceed from the premise that online interactions, as well as many other types of communication, are correlated with interpretational horizons, which include specific value domains, attitudes and prejudices (Madisson 2016a, 9). The relation between online and offline spheres should be understood as an intertwined realm, because those who meet in online interactions usually are not personas created for one-time identity-games but subjects who have "histories, social-locatedness in various structures, demographics, epistemological standpoints, etc." and what happens on the Internet significantly influences how people experience life when they are not online (Jurgenson 2012, 85).

The structure of the book

In the first part of the book we explain and expand on our main concepts, such as semiotic conflict, information conflict, strategic narrative, semiotic logic of conspiracy theory, etc. We treat conspiracy theories as strategic narratives. In this book, a strategic narrative is defined as "a means by which political actors attempt to construct a shared meaning of the past, present, and future of international politics to shape the behavior of domestic and international actors" (Miskimmon et al. 2017, 6). As any narrative, conspiracy narratives are characterised by the presence of antagonists, protagonists, concrete goals and activities making reaching those goals possible, spatial and temporal relationships, etc. We also discuss problems accompanying conspiracy theories spreading on social media, first and foremost questions arising in connection with deliberate shaping of information streams. This is why we expand the conspiracy narrative with Umberto Eco's conception of the *Model Reader* that allows the researcher to study which semiotic strategies have been used in constructing the audiences targeted in the strategic conspiracy narratives, as well as the unity of the aims the narrative pursues.

In the second part of the book we analyse the strategic use of conspiracy narratives based on the theoretical frame outlined in Part I, and observe three areas: the discourses of politics, marketing, and alternative knowledge. In our examples, we focus on the conspiracy theories that depict the Hungarian Jewish billionaire investor George Soros as an omnipotent villain. We admit that such conspiracy theories often emerge spontaneously, as it were, at the grassroots level, yet there are numerous examples in which different strategic actors skilfully use these theories in order to amplify their own messages and influence the audience's perception of the situation. What is central in our treatment is the question of conflict construction as the strategic core of conspiracy theories, as proceeding from the mode of shaping the audience or the targeted model reader will depend on the peculiarities of the conflict. We treat constructing the conflict between the own and the alien in the framework of cultural semiotics (modelling the relations of *culture–anti-culture, culture–non-culture*) (Lotman, Uspenskij 1978), Ernesto Laclau's theory of hegemony (2005),[1] Chantal Mouffe's (2005) notion of *agonistic logic* and Michel Foucault's notion of *subjugated knowledge* (1980). In the context of subjugated knowledge, the main research question is: how are conspiracy theories used in order to deprecate/demonise dominant institutionalised knowledge? These kind of conspiracy theories often rely on socio-cultural myths, popular plots, historical narratives and religious beliefs.

In the final chapter, we explain conspiracy theories' potential to catch attention, bring along affective reactions in the target audience and cause cascades of sharing on social media against the background of contemporary information overload. More specifically, we bring out how the strategic disseminators of conspiracy theories construct their messages so that these seem as urgent as possible to the audience and thus require immediate reaction. We also discuss the role of the affordances of social media in amplifying such affective communication. Next, we focus on strategic transmedia storytelling that embraces several modalities and platforms. We explain which techniques are used by strategic actors to evoke curiosity and the immersive experience of the story, and how they create cohesion between different story entries. After that, we demonstrate how, in transmedial conspiracy narratives, semantic gaps and triggers function via which the model reader can be led towards desired associations and, at first glance, irreconcilable levels of meaning can be united.

Note

1 On syntesis of cultural semiotics and Laclau's theory of hegemony see also Ventsel (2009a, 2011, 2014) and Selg and Ventsel (2008, 2010, 2020).

Part I
Theoretical framework

1 Semiotic conflicts in strategic communication

We have all probably met conspiracy theories that try to provide explanations to different social, cultural or economic problems. Usually this is accompanied by the reduction of a complex problem to a simple scheme. Such simplifying clarity that is characteristic of conspiracy theories can be better understood in the framework of the concept of *conflict*, for conspiracy theories are commonly characterised by a simple explanatory scheme: someone has been deprived of something or it has been taken from them. What is important is the existence of at least two parties – the victims and the perpetrators who cause their suffering. This work conceptualises such conflicts first and foremost as semiotic ones, i.e. conflicts on the level of meaning-making, and discusses them in the framework of information conflicts and strategic communication.

The following chapters introduce the key notions in our study: *semiotic conflict*, *information conflict* and *strategic narrative*. We position and define these from the point of view of (cultural) semiotics. We also explain methodological difficulties arising in social media research in connection with how to analyse and differentiate the potentially strategically motivated discourse from strategically non-motivated discourse in social media communication.

Conceptualising the conflict of meanings

The terminology of social theories includes terms such as *social hierarchies, distribution of resources, group belonging/exclusion*, etc. What unites these concepts is the fact that they all describe social life as in principle open to inequality, which in its turn is the basis for the diversity of conflicts. In a public discussion concerning any topic, consensus may prove to be the ideal, the final aim with which avoid conflict, but the starting point of discussion is still a conflict or the potential possibility of a conflict. Situations may occur in which social tensions appear to be un-relievable, and in such cases one of the possible ways of mitigating the inequality is the amplification of the conflict that will result in earlier social relationships becoming transformed and replaced with new ones. True, this usually lays a basis for the emergence of a new inequality. Examples can be found in the bloody cataclysms that have followed the realisation of different revolutionary utopias. Conspiracy theories have often played an important role in the amplification of such conflicts, for instance during the French Revolution when King Louis XVI was met with accusations of high treason and of collaborating with foreign powers, or the tales circulating in pre-revolution Russia concerning Rasputin's links with Germany.

In a comprehensive analysis of peacebuilding, Lisa Schrich proposes understanding conflict in three dimensions. First, there is the material dimension that consists of conflict related to land or material resources that are in demand. Second, there is the social dimension, based on a complex interaction between communication, relationships and social interactions. This conflict is framed by social hierarchies, status, social positions, etc. And, third, the symbolic dimension "focuses on how people's worldview shapes how they understand and make meaning of the world, and in particular, conflict. It brings attention to the perceptual, emotional, sensual, cultural, and identity-driven aspects of conflict" (Schrich 2005, 32).

In this book, we shall not reduce the emergence of conflict to an inequality of the social or the material basis, which is why we do not propose studying the possible reasons for the spreading of conspiracy theories caused by economic or social hierarchies as our aim. First and foremost, we concentrate on the symbolic level of conflict as we are interested in the ways of discursive representation, shaping and solving of social conflicts in the course of communicative action. Here, we proceed from the position in discourse theory that all social reality is meaningful and determined by norms, value systems, rules and shared truths that simultaneously shape social practices. It is impossible to access a point from which reality would speak directly, as it were, without discursive mediation. Social relationships, that can always also be viewed as power relationships and thus potentially conflict-laden, are not pre-given, but constructed through social meanings. As Laclau and Mouffe (1985, 153) put it, "The problem of the institution of the social is the definition and articulation of social relations in a field criss-crossed with antagonism" and it is discourse in which "objectivity as such is being constructed" (Laclau 2005, 68). At this point it is important to emphasise that we do not wish to participate in the classic debate between realists and idealists. According to an apt example given by Laclau and Mouffe, it does not make sense to deny the existence of an earthquake. Yet whether the meaning attributed to the earthquake is the wrath of God or that of a natural disaster will depend on the discursive structuration, the formation of discourse (Laclau, Mouffe 1985, 108). We claim the same in this book – while studying conspiracy theories in the framework of semiotics of conflict we shall not reduce the reasons for their emergence to an essentialist basis, be it material inequality or the specificity of human psyche (paranoia), but will treat it as a discursive phenomenon via which the economic and social aspects will become meaningful.

Thus, it is possible to view the emergence of a conflict as the result of a mutual influence of several economic, social and cultural factors, yet not as reducible to these. What is more, the symbolic level does not mediate conflicts, but can be their source, as each order creating a socio-semiotic system or discourse will exclude other meaningful orders and thus serve as a potential trigger of conflict. At the time of contemporary information overload the ways in which some topics are served in the media to catch the audiences' attention is of decisive importance. In addition to the reproduction of a discourse, an "attractively packaged" treatment of a topic – and emphasising a conflict usually is an attention magnet – creates the possibility of a new discourse emerging as other, potentially important, topics remain in the shadow. If "reality" is revealed to us in discourse, the following questions will be raised: how discourses are being produced through signs, and whether there is anything in the structure of the sign and in sign systems that turns them from bare means of discourse formation and communication to the reason for conflicts potentially developing.

The ontology of the semiotic conflict

Drawing on one of the founders of semiotics, Ferdinand de Saussure, the sign can be interpreted as an in-system correlate between the signified and the signifier (2011). The conception of the sign by the important founder of another semiotic tradition, Charles Sanders Peirce (1932), proceeds from the tertiary division of the sign – the object, the representamen and the interpretant – and the transformation of the relations between them in the semiotic process in which a certain ambivalence of meaning has been encoded via the interpretant. Yet in the case of both Saussure's and Peirce's models of signs, we can see the possibility of the sign itself positioning as the source of a conflict: the sign's relation with the mediated "reality" has been developing in different communication situations over time and rendered socially "naturalised", although it is essentially contingent and could in principle be different. It is true that this will not lead us to a better understanding of the connections between meaning-making and conflict, but only indicates that every signification process is potentially a source of conflict as well as of power relations (Ventsel 2009a, 2011; see also Marchart 2007, 5–6). In order to better understand which factors contribute to semiosis and how this can lead to a semiotic conflict we need to regard meaning-making in the context of communicative activity.

According to cultural semiotics, that rather proceeds from a Saussurean view of meaning-making, sign systems such as natural languages, languages of art (literature, painting, theatre, etc.), ideologies, cultures, etc., are immanently organised structures. It is only structured organisation that allows us to speak of meaningful information that opposes disorganisation (Lotman et al. 2013, 54–55). It is true that it is only from an internal point of view of a meaningful unit (e.g. a culture, community, etc.) that it looks like "chaos" or seems not so organised. From an external point of view, which can be, e.g., the researcher's position, in most cases it is information organised in a way that is different from other perspectives (ibid.).

At the same time there is no mechanism in any sign system that would guarantee the latter's functioning in isolation, for sign systems only operate in unity, relying on one another (ibid). The particular identity of a meaningful unit is formed in the context in which it functions and enters into contact with other semiotic systems. Being thus defined helps the semiotic unit (which can be the conspiracy theory of Rasputin's plotting mentioned above or a broader ideological discourse) to differentiate between the semiotically own and the semiotically alien, filters outside information and sets off the mechanism of re-processing outside information into the inside (Lotman 2005, 208–209). In the course of such a process, the identity of the semiotic unit is shaped and it is characteristic of meaning-making that in a situation in which two semiotic units come into contact they immediately proceed from a situation of reciprocal neutrality into a situation of reciprocal complementarity – they start to cultivate their own specific character and mutual contrast (Lotman 1997, 11). Thus the "chaos" that is considered alien from an internal point of view is not always original, uniform and equal to itself but is as actively created by humans as is the cultural field (Lotman et al. 2013, 54). It is always the result of relationality, and what various conspiracy theories or ideological discourses will turn out to be like will in several respects depend on the context of their spreading and the functions they have in communication (see also Selg, Ventsel 2020).

In the context of the information war discussed in this book the relationality introduced above emerges in the descriptions of the antagonists and protagonists of conspiracy theories and the goals of their activities. The identity of a semiotic unit (protagonist, antagonists, event, etc.) is not characterised by a set of unchanging authentic or primordial properties, but rather defined through constantly developing processes of meaning-making, transformed in interplay with an altering socio-cultural context (Campbell 2008, 410). The processes of identity creation are not predetermined by certain essential (material or social) factors, but suggest the making of semiotic choices, as well as a degree of contingency and unpredictability. The cultural semiotic approach sees the processes of identity creation as an integral part of communication and follows an anti-essentialist perspective which treats identities as a matrix of difference (Madisson 2016b, 22).

Such a process of identity-creation can be observed in the framework of various intertwined functions. In addition to differentiating between the own and the alien, as well as identity shaping, semiotic units have the function of transmitting and storing information and creating new meanings (Lotman 1988a). A precondition for the realisation of the functions is the existence of memory, as without it no dialogue could possibly arise. Cultural semiotics does not view memory as a passive space where information packages could be stored, but it is an active (re)generator of meanings (Lotman 1988a, 55). A tension of meaning-making arises in situations in which "[c]ulture is united with its past by memory generates not only its own future, but also its own past, and in this sense is a mechanism that counteracts natural time" (Lotman, Uspenskij 1984, 28). Memory should thus be observed first and foremost as a dynamic semiotic mechanism that becomes activated in the interaction of codes and texts in concrete acts of communication.

Although in each process of meaning-making these three functions (communication, memory, innovation) operate simultaneously, in particular situations we can speak of the prevailing of one or another function. Semiotic conflicts develop in the communication process in which, in addition to the essential overlap of sign systems, tension also arises due to the differences in the functions of semiotic systems. For different interpreters, the goal of conspiracy theories can be seen as either the retaining the status quo or launching a new system of meanings and social changes. For instance the repeated addresses of the Hungarian premier Viktor Orbán against the presumed conspiracy organised by George Soros, that is purportedly undermining the state and national unity, serve the Orbán's aim of retaining his position and legitimising stricter measures against NGOs. Soros's Jewish ethnicity and his image as a financial magnate can be used strategically in constructing a common figure of the enemy, in contrast to which the populist "people" is created. However, the same conspiracy theory makes it possible for Orbán's opponents in the political struggle to show him as a ridiculous enemy of democracy and an anti-Semite.

Naturally, not every tension will develop into a real conflict and not every conflict has been shaped consciously, but may arise from the coincidence of arbitrary circumstances, carelessness or ignorance of the context. However, such contingent conflicts can be made later strategic use of; we shall demonstrate such conspiracy theories in the examples given in Part II of this book. The realisation of the conflict will be determined by the domination of a function in communication that suppresses other modes of meaning-making and modelling of the world. As we can read in *The Theses of Semiotics of Culture*, "particular importance is attached to questions of the hierarchical structure of the languages of culture, of the distribution of spheres among them, of cases in which these spheres intersects or merely border upon each other" (Lotman et al. 2013, 53).

In this subchapter we outlined the nature of semiotic conflicts that are potentially present in a latent form in each meaning-making process. In view of the discussion conducted in this book we need to move further and speak of information conflict. This is based on the ontology of the semiotic conflict, but presumes a deliberate shaping of the conflict, a strategic nature of some communicative activities.

Information conflicts and information warfare

The term "information conflict" is used to "encompass both military and non-military applications of information warfare tactics and conflict will include strategic information security and influence operations" (van Niekerk, Maharaj 2013, 1163). Traditionally, information conflicts have been treated in the framework of information war in the field of the military. Information war can be defined as "all actions taken to defend the military's information-based processes, information systems and communications networks and to destroy, neutralize or exploit the enemy's similar capabilities within the physical, information and cognitive domains" (Brazzoli 2007, 219).[1]

Conceptions of information war evolved in several countries starting from the second half of the twentieth century. In such a war, information is the goal, the resource and the means. To conduct information war, special information weapons are devised that depend on the goals aspired to and the nature of the informational environment. According to the Danish expert on information war, Thomas Elkjær Nissen, the informational environment consists of three interconnected dimensions that interact with one another: the physical, the informational and the cognitive. The informational dimension specifies the physical dimension, indicating where and how information is being collected, processed, stored, spread and protected. In the cognitive dimension, information is forwarded and received, as well as reacted to and acted upon (Nissen 2015, 24). On this level people's reactions and decisions are generated that those who issue the messages wish to affect with their information weapons. The information weapons can be, for instance, means of radio-electronic communication; means of program-electronic communication, i.e. those that concern software and hardware; and informational-psychological means. The former two are targeted against technology, while the means of the latter kind are employed first and foremost to influence people's decision-making processes. Physical, informational and cognitive dimensions intermingle, but analytically this tertiary division can still offer a framework for understanding the structure of the informational battlefield and provide a usable toolkit for "understanding the information 'battle-space' and how both technology (including social network media), processes (technological and human) and content (images, words and the perception of observable action) fit together and create effects" (Nissen 2015, 25). In this book we mostly focus on the third, cognitive dimension.

Although information warfare has traditionally been considered as a military concept, Blaise Cronin and Holly Crawford (1999) and Winn Schwartau (1996) have shown it to be relevant as regards social, corporate and personal spheres. Saara Jantunen, researcher of information warfare of the Finnish Defence Forces, remarks that according to the principles of hybrid warfare influencing the opponent, e.g. economically, with cyber attacks and with psychological operations, organised influencing activities may mean that information warfare need not even be part of conventional direct military operations, but the influencing may take place over mass media, social media, conversations between ordinary civilians and in other non-military environments. Thus, information war does not leave the impression of being an activity of the state but is conducted with the help of civilians and bystanders (Jantunen 2018, 37). Therefore, employing a unidirectional behaviourist model that treats communication as "a mouthful given to the target auditorium from above, intended to tease out a desired reaction in the auditorium" (Jantunen 2018, 225) will not suffice to explain contemporary information conflicts. In a web-based and networking world, communication cannot be reduced to a chain of stimuli and reactions, but is asymmetrical, pluri-directional and interactional.

In his book *Out of the Mountains: The Coming Age of the Urban Guerrilla* (2013) the conflict theorist David Kilcullen identifies three reasons for the change in nature of conflicts. Today's conflicts are more urban; technology has changed the nature of warfare; and democratisation of technology gives different social groups the strength to participate in them. Thanks to the leap in the development of information and communication technology and its relatively cheap cost, nearly all of us can access the interpretation and production of information flows. The three characteristics pointed out by Kilcullen create conditions that, taken as a whole, magnify the role of social media in future conflicts where wars will be fought more for local power, money and control over the decision processes of the population. Nissen (2015, 9) characterises the complex influence structure of today's communication as follows: "Effects that support the goals and objectives of the multiple actors 'fighting' in the social network media sphere, including influencing perceptions of what is going on, can, in turn, inform decision-making and behaviours of relevant actors." Thus, one of the most significant reasons in reconsidering the conception of *information war* is the increasing role of social media in interpersonal communication. The concepts of *information war* and *war* in general do not only point at conventional confrontations between states, but sooner concern identity and identity claims based on the logic of inclusion and exclusion (ibid.).

In our book, we also treat conspiracy theories in the conceptual framework of expanded information war and information conflicts, in which the possible aims of their application can include marketing, establishing alternative knowledge or undermining an opposing political regime. Through shaping information conflicts, adversaries or competitors can directly assault or strategically undermine the opponent's assets (Denning 1999). In an age of social media, the speed of reaching audiences is a significant parameter of information culture. Attribution of meaning to any particular piece of information and checking its credibility is becoming ever more difficult and requires increasingly more resources. At the same time, the motives behind people's sharing of bits of information that seem exciting and intriguing, although of dubious value, cannot be boiled down to just their evil plans of fanning a conflict or a desire to increase the number of clicks. As a rule, entertainment aspects and the marking of community belonging (Ventsel, Madisson 2017, 99) also play a role here. Still, it is possible to use such pieces of information for strategic purposes, either in generating and directing an information conflict or, to the contrary, in devising one's own protective strategy. Social media can also be used to damage or improve the reputation of an organisation or an individual; Gaines-Ross (2010) labels this phenomenon, "reputation warfare". The emission of the WikiLeaks materials on the Internet in 2010, or the exposing on the Web of nearly 11.5 million documents leaked from the Panamanian law firm Mossack Fonseca, in which documents torn out of their contexts were used in new communication situations with aims different from the original ones (see Singer, Brooking 2018), might serve as good examples here.

The semiotic point of view presented in this book proves all the more useful considering that social media encompasses a diverse range of communication styles, including multimedia and short messages, and connects a wide range of actors; it is a complex network. The internet researcher Andrew Chadwick (2009) claims that the emergence of hybrid media systems creates a new onto-logical situation in which the social is constituted by "simultaneous integration and fragmentation". Conscious shaping of the conflict of cognitive dimension is based on the mechanisms and functions referred to above, as well as an awareness of the peculiarities of social media communication. In the following subchapter we shall focus on some of these.

On the specificity of the informational influencing on social media

As pointed out in the Introduction, different parties in information conflicts may realise the multi-faceted potential of conspiracy theories in the strategic shaping and directing of the opinion climate. The explanatory frames of conspiracy the-ories offer simple solutions and they successfully catch the attention of the target audience; thus, they can fruitfully be applied as a strategic narrative whose aim is to shape the perception of the situation by its target audience and the latter's behaviour. Conspiracy theories make it possible to fortify communal identity but also to create confusion and sow distrust regarding certain information and institutions, cause fear and suspicion, and amplify confrontations.

Several researchers of today's information wars have identified that, in the past decade, influencing directed against democratic countries and their citizens has mostly been taking place via social media (Nissen 2015; Singer, Brooking 2018). Social media is an important theatre of information conflicts as it makes it possible for strategic actors: (1) to retain their loyal supporters and, as it were, shape and groom them as an audience; (2) to win the support of neutral audiences; (3) to undermine opponents by disseminating one's own narrative (see Nissen 2015, 84–85). Thus Twitter, Facebook, YouTube, Reddit and other platforms of participatory media have evolved into the main channels via which coordinated misinformation is being distributed in time of peace. The influencing on social media is particularly effective in latent or early phases of conflicts and crises, for then the audiences are not in a heightened critical mindset nor yet suspicious of possible misinformation (Nissen 2015, 101). Below, the adaptation of contemporary influencing to the possibilities of communication and the signification possibilities of social media will be discussed in more detail. We rely on several weighty studies on the opinion climate and meaning-making tendencies of social media, and highlight some reasons why strategic conspiracy narratives are particularly well-suited to the narrating practices of social media.

The role of social media influencers in the shaping of conflict

In an era of participant media, the diversity of public platforms for discussion has diversified considerably and speakers need not depend on journalism as a mediating gatekeeper in order to reach a potentially large audience. The paradox of social media, however, lies in the fact that the number of opinion holders and discussion platforms has multiplied to such a degree that it is quite likely that any particular posting will not be noticed by nearly anyone against the background of a general flood of information. This information overload has increased the relevance of focusers or filters of attention, which can be institutions, individual mediators (e.g. social media micro-celebrities) or algorithms (e.g. those that mark trending themes), that can bring attention to a certain topic or an event (Tufekci 2013, 856). On social media, visibility and virality belong to the most desirable resources in the name of which different interest groups compete; at the same time, it is also a "force that can be manipulated and sustained by just a few influential social media accounts" (Singer, Brooking 2018, 335). For instance, such super-spreaders played an immensely important role in pushing the Pizzagate conspiracy theories onto the pages of alt-right social media (Singer, Brooking 2018). It is important to notice that texts gaining quick popularity are also supported by platform algorithms which "drive stories quickly, gaining attention to virality and thus further attention" (O'Loughlin et al. 2017, 34).

The main risk connected with social media influencers lies in the fact that they wield great power in the development of the social meaning of certain topics, but their aims and principles of acting often remain hidden from audiences. In the formation of the meaning of contemporary conflicts such influencers certainly play a key role; their primary aim is to win the visiting loyalty and trust of a segment of the audience by frequent and interesting postings. Social media influencers bring together information related to particular topics and many (first and foremost personified) influencers often also dispense instructions as to how this information should be interpreted. The social media accounts of particular influencers, and the web pages and groups related to these, serve as a discussion space where the contents posted can be discussed with the posters themselves as well as their audiences. Such influencers can participate in deliberately coordinated networks of influencing activities and be engaged in the dissemination of strategic talking points dictated from above, as it were, but their posting activities can also be self-started, aiming at the advancement of personal brands, i.e. increasing personal popularity. Often, they are doing both.

The other main aim of these mediators is advocating their strategic narratives with audiences and making their content self-evident, as well as self-spreading or viral via social media. Several researchers of contemporary dis- and misinformation campaigns have noted that, in most cases, traditional media also plays a role in concrete fake news or conspiracy theories becoming viral, although, as a rule, it does not affirm the content of the information, but notes its wide spreading on social media (Jantunen 2018; Nissen 2015). At the same time it is important to note that even though dominant media outlets indicate that it is a "conspiracy theory" or an unchecked claim spreading on social media when it comes to such content, the popularity of the particular social media thread(s) will experience a noticeable rise after the appearance of such media coverage (Silverman 2015, 3). Thus, the aim of social media influencers is to create posts that are sufficiently intriguing and absorbing to trigger an extensive flood of shares, which, in turn, would increase the likelihood of getting over the threshold of traditional media outlets (this is most easily accomplished in the case of tabloid newspapers).

Side by side with the growth of the new type of influencers and the appearance of the logic of self-perpetuating virality, it is important to highlight the unprecedentedly high proportion of information practices that are directed at co-experiencing and expressing an immediate reaction, in order to understand the communication and meaning-making tendencies characteristic of social media. The popularity of widespread reactions and of the copying and sharing functions on numerous social media platforms is seen as connected to the discussion of social media becoming more affect- or emotion-based and less argumented (see Andrejevic 2013; Dean 2010; Harsin 2014, 2015; Papacharissi 2014; van Dijck 2013). A large portion of the posts on the timelines of social media groups or various users is made up of texts consisting of emojis, reaction-GIFs and content that has been published earlier, the function of which is generally neither the discussion of the statements made by the conversation partner nor offering new examples or points of discussion. Such postings rather express an awareness of a particular topic and the intensity of one's interest in it and emotional reactions to it. They make it possible for users to participate in discussions without taking specific articulated stands (Madisson, Ventsel 2016a, 343–344).

The researchers of misinformation campaigns on social media have noted that in order to achieve the greatest possible number of 'like'-s and 'share'-s, strategic messages are often packaged as infotainment (Nissen 2015, 50; Singer, Brooking 2018). They are equipped with entertaining elements (humorous memes), for instance, stories of strong human interest about victims suffering from wrongdoing or heroes fighting injustice, as well as sensationalism and content appealing to shock value. The latter criteria are perfectly met by conspiracy theories as these attribute extreme malice and amorality to famous and influential people or institutions. For instance, the Pizzagate conspiracy theory that sparked major engagement on social media connected Hillary Clinton with a secret network of Satanists and paedophiles. It is important to note that a trigger for sharing such posts is not only concern and fear of conspiracies, but an important role is also played by the "kitsch entertainment value of conspiracism as a hip, alternative stance" (Butter, Knight 2016, 5), as well as the wish to test the reactions of one's network of friends. The emotionally saturated gossip that has arisen around conspiracy narratives such as Pizzagate has value as an influencing recourse, even if the audience is aware of its dubious truthfulness. Namely, it makes it possible to playfully introduce and ingrain strategically important explanation schemes, as well as familiarise the audience with the code repertory necessary for the comprehension of future messages. Studies have shown that even if conspiratorial claims are dismissed, the mere exposure to conspiratorial discourse will create distrust of official explanations (Lewandowsky et al. 2017, 355; see Jolley, Douglas 2013).

Affective narrating practices and affective communities

As mentioned above, influencing on social media is particularly effective in an emerging conflict situation, when the official account of the events still contains gaps or contradictions. In cases such as, for instance, terrorist attacks, unexpected data leaks or natural disasters, social media is the main source of obtaining information and it is then that influencers disseminating strategic narratives will be able to establish the explanation frames they are offering. Legal scholars and communication researchers Cas Sunstein and Adrian Vermeule have identified that after unexpected socially significant events conspiracy cascades are often unleashed on the Internet that explain the events in a language that is generally understandable and cast doubts on previously accepted views or institutions that had been perceived as trustworthy. Such cascades of conspiracy theories offer a certain solution to the information vacuum of the official channels, but their more important task is triggering intense emotions (e.g. fear, indignation and disgust) and releasing collective affect (Sunstein, Vermeule 2009, 215). Internet researchers have noticed that in periods when crises are unleashed, affective communication takes over on social media as people share their impressions about the degree of their sense of feeling disturbed as well as their emotions and associations via tweets, reactions and other phatic postings (see Dean 2010; Papacharissi 2014). At such moments, social media functions as a point of convergence of affects and as a structure catalysing a common expression of affect (Prøitz 2017, 10). The importance of such affective communication practices lies in the fact that in the course of such practice, a cognitive atmosphere that will surround the topics and a rudimentary way of preliminary labelling of their collective meaning will be shaped (Papacharissi 2016, 311). The basis for such affective communication lies in the expression of the joint recognition that some aspects are of key importance in understanding certain events, but that these are not yet divided into clearly distinct meaningful units, but seem intuitively meaningful for people. Such making of connections on the basis of strong emotions and affective recognition and weak or even non-existent (rational) argumentation has been called a collective gut feeling or visceral response (Andrejevic 2013; Marmura 2014; van Dijck 2013).

Sunstein and Vermeule (2009, 216) have noted that affective conspiracy cascades have a direct connection with group polarisation and the formation of communicative echo chambers. Their conclusion has been corroborated by quantitative studies dedicated to conspiracy theories spreading on social media (Bessi et al. 2015a, 2015b; Del Vicario et al. 2016). The affective common core can turn into a basis for creating a more permanent community. Such communities are often characterised by selective exposure to conspiracy cascades based on a collective visceral response and the continuous looking for validation to convictions they already hold (selective exposure and confirmation bias). Sunstein and Vermeule (2009, 217) emphasise that in the formation of echo chambers of conspiracy theories and amplification of the belief in conspiracies, influencers who initiate interactions that will "lead people toward a more extreme point in line with what group members initially believed" play a major role.

Information conflicts and strategic narratives

"Rewritings of history", "accusations of Russophobia", "alternative facts" and many other similar keywords point at a tendency that can be characterised as a battle for meanings, as a means of enforcing soft power. This is by no means a new phenomenon. In post-revolution Russia, the poet Vladimir Majakovski (2013, 217), a leading figure of Agitprop,[2] wrote on the role of the word in mobilising the masses: "The word is commander of the human army"; social theories have been discussing ideological battles at the centre of social analyses already for centuries. Yet it seems that, in comparison with earlier periods, a significant constituent part of today's conflicts (including military conflicts) is made up by audiences who have a say in the result of the conflict. Noticeably, the conflicts are fashioned by the meanings constructed in the course of interactions (e.g. logical as well as emotional debates, etc.) taking place in communication networks (both physical and virtual) (Nissen 2015, 32). Information conflicts can be consciously shaped in the course of coordinated action of state or non-state actors. Thus today, when a major proportion of information is circulating on the Internet, we typically meet cases of economic sabotage, e.g. stealing of product development programmes or other spying on trade secrets. In addition, as was indicated above, the character of war has changed significantly. Often a conflict can be shaped and directed on the cognitive level without any attending activities in the other, physical and informational dimensions, of the information environment. Thus, various influence operations can be seen as an extension of military psychological operations in order to cover public affairs, corporate communication, perception management and similar activities (Larson et al. 2009). For instance, citizen journalists can document battles and potentially influence the agenda of the media and political discourses via this documentation. New media often receives its input from the social media used by citizen journalists to publicise their work. This book primarily focuses on the cognitive level of the information environment. We explain how conspiracy theories are being employed in the battle "for the hearts and minds" of audiences.

An important strategy of undermining and influencing is the creation of "information fog". In order to create "information fog", select pieces of information, contradictions, fabrications, misleading information and downright lies are used. In cases where "information fog" is created successfully, the audience will not be capable of differentiating between truth and falsehood. Thus Donald Trump can label media coverage that is critical of him simply as "fake news", which is why it is not fake news as such, but the use of the label to counteract the position of the opponent that has become a kind of strategy (Farkas, Schou 2018). This is a device of context directing, with the aim to make it more difficult for the audience to make well-considered decisions. Such activity will be more effective when it appears as a strategy used in a deliberate and coordinated information war. Thus Jantunen (2018, 204) points out that if "in Western thinking the aim of information war is to unite the target audience and win it over to one's own side", then "in Russian thinking it suffices if confrontations and controversies appear in the target audience so that it will not function as united any more". Different English-language Russian propaganda channels, such as Russia Today, Sputnik, and the social media trolls supporting these, present a challenge that Western governments have to deal with when psychologically protecting their nations.

Another option is linked with the presentation of an opposing narrative that attempts to fashion a public system of meanings and to influence the audience's decision-making processes while remaining hidden. It is true that the emission of strategic narratives (that may be deliberately contradictory) into the media, and disseminating them there, can bring about an effect similar to that of information fog – a deliberate disorientation of the audience. In the following, we shall discuss the concept of the strategic narrative and its functions in information conflicts.

Strategic narrative

The concept of the strategic narrative was first introduced in Lawrence Freedman's (2006) paper, which observes how narrative can be used strategically to challenge opponents in military conflict. Freedman treated the strategic narrative as a tool with which to problematise the legitimacy of the powers of the (military) enemy. Yet strategic narratives may include also the justification of policy objectives or policy responses to economic or security crises, the formation of international alliances, or the rallying of domestic public opinion (Antoniades et al. 2010, 5–6). The expansion of the field of usage of the strategic narrative concept is closely related to the reconceptualisation of one of its basic categories – the actor – in which it is not treated as a term belonging strictly to the military field. It is now open to those beyond the state (Miskimmon et al. 2013, 30–59) and avoids valorising any particular actor: "the concern with who narrates and who is perceived to be narrating and what difference this makes to processes of power and influence in international relation" (O'Loughlin et al. 2017, 52). Therefore, several authors have been developing the conception of the strategic narrative further in the framework of international relations and foreign policy analysis (Miskimmon et al. 2013, 2017; Ringsmose, Børgesen 2011; Dimitriu, De Graaf 2016), info warfare (Nissen 2015; Ventsel et al. 2019), as well as in conflict studies (Wetoszka 2016). In this book we attempt to broaden the field in which this term can be applied to marketing communication and the sphere of alternative knowledge. In our opinion this is relevant primarily due to the growth of the role of social media in shaping public opinion and the frequent participation of several actors beyond the state in shaping and magnifying the narratives circulating on social media.

To put it broadly, the interpretive structure or narrative helps the audiences attribute a meaning to what is going on. Lotman has noted that narrating about an event presupposes the articulation of logical and causal relations – subsidiary events are arranged into a fixed storyline; simultaneous events that need not even be connected are reorganised into a consistent and cohesive chain. Telling a story entails segmentation of the flow of experience, which has been perceived as continuous, into many concrete units which are thereafter ordered in a definite way: temporal and causal relations are created with other elements of the story, and meaningfulness is attributed to the whole story (see Lotman 2000, 170). Narratives are inextricably accompanied by interpretation. There are no "true stories", as events are identified and stories are told from specific perspectives linked to specific interests; they are not found in the world in a ready-made form (White 2003, 9). But what characteristics make a narrative a strategic narrative?

Strategic narratives are characterised by their function and intentionality; that is, they are accompanied by a deliberate intention to shape the meanings of conflicts in a way desired. As a rule, via their strategic narratives, actors attempt to justify their action to audiences and influence the latter's behaviour (O'Loughlin et al. 2017, 50). Strategic narratives can be described as "means by which political actors attempt to construct a shared meaning of the past, present, and future of international politics to shape the behaviour of domestic and international actors" (Miskimmon et al. 2017, 6). Strategic narratives usually establish the identity of the active actor (*who we are?*), a desired destination (*what we want to achieve?*), the obstacles related to it and the recommended way of overcoming these obstacles (Miskimmon et al. 2013, 3).

One of the primary functions of strategic narratives is it offer "a framework through which conflicts' past, present and future can be structured in order to help establish and maintain power in the international system and shape the context and the system itself" (Nissen 2015, 45). They create a context that organises various information fragments and guides the meaning-making of the (social) media audience. "Strategic narratives may be designed to elicit particular behavior by referring to historical stories in a complicated sort of interplay and entanglement" (Miskimmon et al. 2017, 1). Thus, strategic narratives have to take into account the target group's views and expectations at the moment, while being aware of topics that are sensitive from the perspective of the audience's identity. It is also important to be familiar with the meaning-making practices of the audience, e.g. whether it has rather adopted an image-based or a verbal logic of framing messages; what types of communication styles are usual, etc. Knowing the target audience and the particular communication context helps to activate the meaning-making mechanisms in the audience's memory, if required, that can be used to shape and direct the interpretation paths of the targeted audience. Thus, influencing often employs very emotional and/or contradictory themes, combining events that the target group knows (or, actually, interpretations of these) with others that have been orchestrated or even fabricated.

From the perspective of the semiotic conflict and the influence of the strategic narrative, the question of which symbols, texts and other discursive phenomena known to the target audience have been used to construct the narrative appears to be as important. According to O'Loughlin et al. (2017, 33) strategic narratives are not so much characterised by an exchange of rational claims but they rather are an unpredictable, textured and recursive set of overlapping ecologies in which history can be mobilised through visuals, symbols and appeals to emotion. Much of this may be unintentional. As James Liu and Denis Hilton point out, symbols in cultural memory function as mediators that create links between the important socio-political events of today and earlier generations and history (Liu, Hilton 2010). As a significant memory mechanism, "symbols carry texts, plot schemas and other semiotic formations from one stratum of culture to another" (Ventsel 2009b, 19). Two aspects are relevant for us here: a symbol retains its invariant nature in the flow of time, yet on the other hand, a symbol correlates actively with its cultural context, is transformed by its influence and transforms it itself (Lotman 2019, 163–164). Thus, symbols and texts important for the audience[3] here fulfil the function of collective cultural memory. In this role, they exhibit, on the one hand, the ability of continuous completion and, on the other, of actualising some aspects of the information saved there, while other aspects are temporarily or fully forgotten (Lotman, Uspenskij 1975; Lotman 2000, 104). This is why texts and symbols that are important from the point of view of particular audience's common memory serve as a powerful and emotional discursive device in strengthening in-group ties, often accompanied by "the exclusion of another cultural group" (Philips DeZalia, Moeschberger 2014, 4). In the framework of conflict theory Rebekah Phillips DeZalia and Scott Moeschberger emphasise the function of symbols as cognitive filters and anchor points for individuals to assimilate and interpret new information in relation to culture. This filter ultimately helps to shape cognitive attributions related to group membership and categorisation. In this way, symbols serve to both enhance and inform social identities strengthening "us/them" and "in-group/out-group" perspectives (Phillips DeZalia, Moeschberger 2014, 4–5). In the case of accelerated communication mediated by social media, the use of such symbols is even more relevant; they function like anchor points whose cognitive reception is based not so much on reflective information processing, but on emotional and often affective identification (Ventsel, Madisson 2017).

Of course, strategic uses of narratives and symbols may not always elicit those results in the audience that the author of the narrative desired. The effect of strategic inducement may greatly depend on the preliminary attunement of the audience to the addresser's intentions, the perceived reliability of the media channel and other contextual variables (Ventsel et al. 2019).

Methodological challenges

Differently from the artistic narratives presented in particular works of literature, non-fictional narratives (including strategic narratives) are often scattered and intertwined. For example, they can pass through different communication channels and texts, varying from news and press releases to social media postings and comments. A single media text can contain several, sometimes contradictory, narratives. Similarly, the real aim is scattered and the actor of the strategic narrative is often hidden in different texts because the success of discursive power (in the current case, of strategic narratives) greatly depends on how its direct aim can be disguised from the audience (Foucault 1977). Therefore, to a certain extent, the unity of the narrative and its aim are always a mental construction created during the analysis.

According to Miskimmon et.al three levels should be differentiated between when analysing strategic narratives: formation, which addresses how narratives are formed by actors; projection, which addresses how narratives are projected (or narrated) and contested in (social) media, by different spokespersons, etc.; and reception, which addresses how narratives are received by targeted audience and how they shape the future actions of the audience (Miskimmon et al. 2017, 9). The present work primarily focuses on the levels of formation and projection. The main methodological problems on these levels mostly concentrate around the deliberate quality of the strategic narratives – how to detect a certain shaper or actor of strategic narratives and approach the intentional (and sometimes manipulative) formation and projection of narratives circulating on social media, and how to analyse the targeting of the audience? In the context of social media, it is more difficult to make claims about the intention of policymakers, journalists and others involved. Critical statements about "malevolent intent or supportive claims about goodwill both appear weak without actual firsthand contact [who is forming strategic narratives – *authors' comment* M-L.M, A.V]" (O'Loughlin et al. 2017, 51). The same problem has been pointed out by Jantunen, according to whom the asymmetry of means of influencing suggests that the agents and their motives will often remain increasingly more unclear in the future. The difficulty in their attribution has been inscribed in the asymmetric means of influencing (Jantunen 2018, 49).

This is why O'Loughlin et al. recommend that we "think imaginatively about constructing extremely systematic analysis of those actors' statements, actions, and reactions and about how inferences about strategic intention can be validated" (2017, 51). We are aware of the difficulties of identifying the intentionality which drives the creation of certain social media content, and elaborate Eco's (2005) concept of *Model Reader/Model Author* and Lotman's concept of *the structure of audience* (1982) in the context of strategic narrative analysis to explain the techniques of targeting an audience that are always related with audience memory, and the problem of intentionality of the actor in social media communication.

The Model Reader and the image of the audience

The basis for influencing via a strategic narrative is the communication between the author, the text and the recipient, and, as was mentioned earlier, (successful) communication presumes that the communication partners have a common component in their memories. For the message to meet the aims desired by the sender, its interpretational aspect has to be "part of its generation mechanism: to generate a text means to trigger a strategy a component of which is foreseeing the other party's moves" (Eco 2005, 61). In the eyes of Eco, the recipient is always postulated as an operator who in a real situation of text interpretation actualises semantic, syntactic, etc., codes, uses meanings known to them earlier, creates links between different parts of the text and intertextual links with other texts. Activity on the part of the reader is added by the author who consciously writes into the text "the unsaid" in addition to what is said (Eco 2005, 57–58). The "unsaid" can consist of what is culturally taken for granted, but also, the other way round, in codes known only to a limited group that make it possible for the members of that group to uncover the text's full meaning potential, while the text remains incomprehensible to those not familiar with the code. In this context, phatic communication of conspiracy theories will be discussed below. It is of considerable importance in communicating on social media, for often the semiotic units that trigger the readers' activity are given as excerpts, not as a clear narrative.

From the point of view of the actor (the term used by Miskimmon et al.) or author (the term used by Eco)[4] of a strategic narrative, taking into consideration such predicting of the possible interpretative moves of the reader and the directing of these is, on the one hand, caused by pragmatic goals. The author wishes that his or her message be understood in a way that suits him or her. On the other hand, another reason lies in the optimisation of communicative activity, for in a situation in which each constituent part of the message has to be defined for the reader, the message would become too extensive and lose the audience's attention. In this connection, Lotman (1982) speaks of two types of text construction that proceed from the image of the audience and are different in principle. First, there are texts that are addressed to any addressee in which the scope of the addressee's memory is constructed as an essential minimum for each speaker of the language (other than that communication and understanding would prove impossible, i.e. speaking would occur in a private language). The memory scope here is impersonal, abstract and only contains a condensed minimum. It is natural that the poorer the memory, the more detailed and expanded the message must be and the less appreciated are ellipses and omissions, the blanks to be filled in, as it were (Lotman 1982). Speaking in the context of the strategic narrative, encoding of the blanks is an indispensable step by the former, for otherwise the reader might detect the manipulation. The other text type, on the other hand, considers the audience as a particular addressee known to the speaker personally (Lotman 1982).[5] In case of both text types it is important that the author of the message form the scope of the memory of the reader, as, after receiving the text of the message, the audience can, thanks to the structure of human memory, recall what was previously unknown to them (Lotman 1982). Thus, on the one hand the author presses on the audience the nature of their memory (helps the reader remember via using certain signs); on the other hand the text still retains an image of the audience (that is potentially hidden in the reader).

In the strategy of text creation, as in any other strategy, the idea of the receiver's (in this case conceived of as the potential audience, the reader of the message) capability of reading the text is crucial. Yet it is important to emphasise that the competence of the receiver does not necessarily equal the competence of the sender. In order to guarantee a decoding that would be as accurate as possible, the author constructs a Model Reader while creating the text, who in decoding the text would depart from a strategy that would be as similar as possible to that of the author of the narrative when creating it. Ideally, the Model Reader should be able to actualise the same competences (codes, context, etc.) as those which the author desires should be actualised when reading the text. Although, on the one hand, the authors presume competence from the Model Reader, on the other hand they establish it themselves. In a typical situation the members of the audience have different and fragmentary bits of memory concerning an event and its possible reasons, which means that the reader lacks sufficient competence regarding some connotations. If the author of the strategic narrative is capable of uniting these bits of memory with an explanation scheme related to a strategic narrative (e.g. conspiracy theory), they can activate a coherent interpretative horizon in the audience, which in its unity has the potential to guide the readers' future interpretative paths. Thus, each text also builds its readers itself (Eco 2005, 63), first by shaping the target audience in a strategic narrative, which will later make it possible to achieve the desired aims via using this narrative.

In addition to the Model Reader, the methodology offered by Eco also makes it possible to analyse the self-images of the sender, i.e. the Model Author. This becomes particularly relevant in cases when the author's position has not been presented explicitly (e.g. deictically, using the first person singular), but is revealed through mediated discourses. In strategic narratives, the author's position is often hidden for its excessive explication could reveal the intentions of the author of the narrative and possible manipulation. In the context of information war, the media texts often refer to "experts" and "former insiders" who confirm the positions of the main narrative. The audience is more likely to trust a critical claim, comment or even media content based on erroneous information if it comes from several sources or if it is being mediated via an authoritative source. Therefore, we can often hear in Russia's English-language media channels such as RT and Sputnik comments critical of the West coming from "a famous German economist", "a recognised member of the European Parliament", "a popular politician, former Foreign Minister" or "a well-known British political analyst". The Model Author of the strategic narrative appears as an in-text role that is pointed at in various ways: through language usage, the function, the role adopted, etc.

According to Eco, the Model Reader and the Model Author are thus types of textual strategy, or a set of succeeding conditions that are textually determined and can thus be studied at the textual level. The conditions of the strategy have to be met for the text to be able to actualise in its potential content (Eco 2005, 69), which is even more important when we speak of the difficulties of attributing intentionality in the case of social media texts, which was discussed earlier. In organising the textual strategy, the question thus arises how the author can presume the competence on part of the audience, which would help the reader to build the text in a way that suits its author. To actualise the discursive strategies of the Model Reader and the Model Author, the reader has to relate to the system of codes and subcodes[6] or other semiotic conditions, some which we are pointing out below:

• *A basic dictionary* that determines the elementary semantic qualities of expressions, that function as minimal meaning postulates or implication rules (Eco 2005, 84). A "married bachelor" is a mistake/error on this elementary level. Each word is accompanied by a certain field of meaning that determines their possible relation with other words belonging to a similar semantic field. What is important in our context is the choice of words that starts to direct the interpretation strategy. The change in the meanings of the terms used as labels in political rhetoric serves as a good example. For example, the term "Russophobia" has been used with both internal and foreign political aims in mind and historically, the power elite of the Kremlin has brought together a great deal of information flows that are negatively disposed towards Russia under the narrative of "Russophobia" (Feklyunina 2013; Peterson 2013). After the breakup of the Soviet Union the accusations of 'Russophobia' have primarily been connected with the expansion of NATO and the European Union, seen as activities directed directly against Russia. Yet it is important that there are attempts to re-contextualise it, shifting it from being against the Kremlin's politics to being against Russian-Slavonic (Eastern) cultures, while discursive attempts at making Russophobia equal with anti-Semitism have been added to this (Darczewska, Żochowski 2015). In case establishing such a link turns out to be successful, it will be able to use it as a strategy in fashioning the construction of the Model Reader that will shape further interpretation paths in the auditorium.

• *Rhetorical and stylistic hyper-encoding* (Eco 2005, 85), in which the reader should be capable of detecting both figurative expressions as well as those with specific stylistic connotations (the author has to take this into consideration in creating the Model Reader). Depending on the character of the target group of the message, the strategic narrative should contain references to the peculiarities of the language use predominant in the audience as well as its slang, the metaphors they would understand, and the audience's expectations regarding the boldness of speech and the representation of the opponents, etc. The narrative of Russophobia that is being skilfully spread by the Russian media exploits the patterns of representing the confrontation between the USA and the USSR from the second half of the twentieth century – the NATO allies of the USA are described as puppets, the citizens of the Baltic countries as Fascists. The latter label was typically used for Estonians, Latvians and Lithuanians while the Baltic nations were occupied by the USSR in 1940–1991 (Ventsel 2016b). On the one hand, this has been caused by the demographic peculiarity of the audience, i.e. part of it is formed by a population who used to live in the Soviet propaganda space. On the other hand, it should be admitted that there is the possibility that semiotic systems and mechanisms of meaning-making, in this case ways of representing the enemy, can become adapted to new circumstances. What changes is the content, yet the basic mechanism of semiosis will be transferred, passed on in time (Ventsel 2007). This can also be observed in case of the following characteristic.

- *Inferences of ordinary scenarios that determine a certain framework of action for participants in narrative* (Eco 2005, 86). For example, the strategic narrative is being managed, based on a scenario of war. In an example of Russophobia, it might point at Russia as a fortress surrounded by enemies. The choice of the scenario shapes the word use that often refers to parallels with war from history (parallels of the Cold War, links between Nazism and Russophobia, or words directly belonging to the war discourse such as "anti-Russophobic front", etc.). Such frames are elements of cognitive knowledge and representations of the "world" that make it possible for us to commit the basic cognitive acts, such as, for instance, the act of perception, linguistic understanding and activities (van Dijk 1998).

- *Inferences of intertextual scenarios*, in which the author of text has to take into account the reader's earlier reading experience and familiarity with genres when constructing the Model Reader (Eco 2005, 88). Differently from the above, here we must tackle rhetorical and narrative schemes that are related to a narrower cultural competence, and the creator of the strategic narrative should avoid such infringement of the genre. The passion story of Russophobia has similarities with religious passion stories. Also here we have a persecuted and humiliated nation (the humiliation accompanying the loss of the Cold War), that is rising from its knees again ("Russia is rising from its knees again") and there is one leader who will make such salvation possible (Alexievich 2016). Exploiting the foundational plots from the cultural memory in the formation of strategic narratives potentially increases the latter's success in finding recognition with audiences, particularly as concerns communication on social media, and in including the audience in creating and disseminating subnarratives that support the main narrative.

- *Ideological hypercoding*, in which the narrative will shape the Model Reader's ideological contingency that will take into consideration the ideological views of the empirical reader (Eco 2005, 92). This can be illustrated by the above example of the strategic narrative of Russophobia concerning and the attempts that have been made to represent it as a new form of anti-Semitism. If such an anti-Semitic connotation becomes established together with the narrative of Russophobia in the interpretational world of the audience, this will open a possibility to ward off criticism from political opponents and an explicit legitimation of Russia's state-endorsed policy.

The list of codes and subcodes is certainly not exhaustive and has been presented in a fairly general manner in this subchapter. Part II will explain them in the context of strategic conspiracy narratives and show their function in the discursive shaping of the conflict, the Model Reader and the Model Author.

The Model Reader and the Model Author as a means of analysing strategic narratives

By adding the Model Author and the Model Reader as text strategic types deductible from an internal analysis of the discourse itself to the treatment of the strategic narrative, we are suggesting one possible solution to the problem formulated at the beginning of the "Methodological challenges" section of this book: who the real actor (be it a policymaker, a marketing strategist or a projector of narratives) is refers to the problem of the intentionality of the actor of the strategic narrative and the question of how to achieve strategical aims which concern targeting the audience. The issue is even more challenging in the case of social media because it enables multi-directional communication in which all people who have access to the Internet and computers (and who are not restricted by other constraints, e.g. censorship) can participate. The content of a social media narrative can spread non-linearly across several platforms, while its *producer's hands are off it*, which means that the audiences themselves are allowed to connect important content points. Thus, it is always difficult to say where someone's strategic calculation ends and where the active narrative creation by the interpreters following their own interpretation paths starts.

In case of the strategic narrative it is important that the aims reached for by the narrative, that to a greater or lesser extent also have to be expressed in the texts circulating on social media, would at the same time shape the unity of the Model Reader. The Model Reader points at the author's understanding of a segment of the audience to which the author has addressed the message (particularly an artistic text) and what Lotman calls the image of the audience (Lotman 1982). Unlike artistic narratives whose author's intention may guide the reader towards multiple paths of parallel reading, the interpretation possibilities of strategic narratives are limited by the nature of conflict and the particular purpose desired by the author, as well as by the specifics of the target audience.

Naturally, the real reader may have some background knowledge as to the intentions of the real actor, e.g. the reader may have a justified suspicion as to the honesty of the creator of the message. Such an attitude on part of the reader that directs the interpretation process is likely to undermine the achieving of the aims aspired to by the strategic narrative, but it also points at the simple fact that the author of the narrative was not able to take into sufficient consideration the background knowledge of the real audience when shaping the Model Reader of strategic narrative. Eco's model poses questions not so much about the author's real intentions, but rather the intentions expressed in the text. It is only these that the audience can agree with or refrain from.

In addition to explaining the problems of the actor's real intentions, the concepts of the Model Author make it possible to avoid the sharp distinction between the actual creator of narratives and the projectors of narratives. As was mentioned above, the problem of attributing agency is one of the most important methodological challenges in communication on social media. In our model, both the real actor as well as the users of social media who develop the narrative further – the narrative magnifiers or projectors in Miskimmon's terms – here make up a single Model Author, whose unity becomes apparent via detecting the aims that they seek to meet. The narrative is made strategic first and foremost by the unity of the aim that can be achieved with its help, not by any particular author behind it. The unity of aims is constructed around the conflict presented in narrative which in its turn is related to the unity of the Model Reader shaped in it or an understanding of a certain segment of the audience who is the first to be influenced. In principle, we could imagine a situation in which the aim of some influencing information action that the Russian state has been wishing for is magnified by a paid army of trolls hired by the US military, or a company whose market share is being threatened is doing the marketing for a competing company. But is such a self-undermining activity really likely?

It does not mean that the differentiation between the actor of a strategic narrative and its amplifier is irrelevant. It is very significant if we want to make somebody take responsibility for manipulations. For example, in the case of the interference in the 2016 US elections we are not so much interested in the possible amplifiers that worked for a St. Petersburg troll factory, called the Internet Research Agency, but in the actors who were giving commands to those trolls, i.e. Russian state authorities. However, this level can be studied with other methodological approaches (e.g. algorithm analysis), while our book presents a framework of qualitative analysis that makes it possible to explain how the social media threads of American users were saturated with conflicts as they were strategically influenced so that people started spreading narratives that possibly overlapped with Russian strategic aims. Eventually, it was Americans who participated in the elections, and not trolls from 55 Savushkina Street, St. Petersburg.[7] Thus, those who formed strategic narratives (Russian state authorities) and those who deliberately (Russian trolls) or inadvertently (American social media users) amplified the narratives worked in a direction which possibly resulted in influencing the election results.

Notes

1 Information warfare can be seen to encompass various other concepts; in this book the following concepts outlined by Brazzoli (2007) are considered: *Network warfare* (or

cyberwarfare) – offensive and defensive actions in relation to information, communications, and computer networks and infrastructure; *Command and control warfare* – actions taken to manage, direct, and coordinate the movement and actions of various forces; seeks to protect this ability in friendly forces and disrupt the ability for an adversary; *Intelligence-based warfare* – actions to degrade an adversary's intelligence cycle while protecting one's own; *Psychological operations* – intended to alter the perceptions of a target audience to be favorable to one's objectives.

2 "Agitprop" is a word for the (communist) political propaganda applied in the Soviet Union that was spread among audiences mostly via popular media, such as literature, games, pamphlets, poems, films, etc. The concept was adopted in Soviet Russia as an abbreviation of the Department of Agitation and Propaganda (*отдел агитации и пропаганды*).

3 The word "symbol" has several different meanings within the humanities, including semiotics (see Todorov 1977; Lotman 2000). In this book we denote by "symbol", content that is in its turn an expression plane for some other content that as a rule is culturally more valuable (Lotman 2000, 104–105). An important characteristic of a symbol is its delimitation, i.e. on the content plane a symbol always is a text that can be differentiated from the surrounding semiotic context (ibid.). Thus, a single sign (e.g. a tricolour flag as a group's identification mechanism), as well as a text (the Bible as a symbol of the Christian religion) can function as a symbol.

4 In this book the concept of *actor of strategic narrative* and Umberto Eco's term *empirical author* are treated as functionally synonymical.

5 Provisionally, we can label the types as text construction types oriented either towards the internal or the external audiences.

6 In a most general way, the code can be defined as a regular correspondence between the content and the expression.

7 The address of a notorious troll factory in St. Petersburg.

2 A semiotic approach to conspiracy theories

Previously, we have explained the shaping and strategic amplification of information conflicts on social media and the possibilities of their semiotic study. In this chapter, the main emphasis is laid on conspiracy theories and the specificity of the meaning-making connected with them. We provide a brief survey of the characteristics and tendencies that researchers from various disciplinary backgrounds have highlighted as the peculiarities of contemporary conspiracy culture dominated by social media. We focus on trends in conspiracy theories that have emerged in connection with the platform affordances of social media (copying, creating of multimodal texts and the possibility of sharing reactions) as well as the peculiarities of spreading conspiracy theories in networks mediating strategic messages. In the following chapter, we introduce communicative functions and provide a semiotic model of conspiracy theories.

Studying conspiracy theories spreading on the Internet

The majority of academic studies dedicated to conspiracy theories in the past decade see the Internet as the most important channel for spreading conspiracy theories. It is believed that this has been the main factor in the explosive growth in the popularity of conspiracy theories and even in their entering the mainstream in Western countries (Ballinger 2011, 3; Bergmann 2018, 154; Soukup 2008, 9). Although bursts of conspiracy theories have been detected as having occurred in culture centuries ago (e.g. the witch hunts of the seventeenth century – see Lotman 2007), it can be claimed with certainty that never before in history have so many people been simultaneously informed about versions of particular conspiracy theories as in this day and age of social media. In addition to spreading conspiracy theories quickly and across geographical boundaries, social media makes it possible to visualise the popularity of any conspiracy theory of interest through likes, shares and comments, and to indicate who among a circle of friends has reacted to it. This information is relevant for it may diminish the risk of being the first in one's circle of acquaintances to bring up the topic of a new and preposterous conspiracy theory and thus deserve the label of a paranoid person (Ventsel, Madisson 2017, 97).

A rather widespread position is that the Internet functions as a Petri dish cultivating conspiracy theories, for the possibility of creating hyperlinks afforded by it suits particularly well the tendency of conspiracy theorists to heap together abundant evidence for the purported existence of a conspiracy and create all possible kinds of associations between phenomena, events or agents that seem to be fairly separate at first glance (see Dean 2002, 97–98; Fenster 2008, 160; Weimann 2003, 348; Soukup 2008, 13). Conspiracy culture that has become adapted to several social media platforms has started to use multimodal means of signification and increasingly often conspiracy theories are finding (audio)visual expression (Ballinger 2011, 245; Soukup 2008, 8). In addition to providing various links, contemporary conspiracy theorists also create intriguing whole texts in the spirit of participant culture or prosumptions based on mixing several web resources (Aupers 2012, 27; Ballinger 2011, 244; Madisson 2016b, 199). Thus, video collages or memes pointing at conspiracies are born. Never before has the visualising of imagined conspiracies been so effortless and easy. Photographic comparisons, zooming in on certain elements and the possibility of creating differences in colour and contrast, allow conspiracy theorists to vividly demonstrate "visual signs of conspiracy" to their audiences (Ballinger 2011, 245; Caumanns, Önnerfson 2020). One of the more widespread practices is the detection and analysis of popular symbols of conspiracy (the triangle, the pyramid, the pentagram, the all-seeing eye, special hand signs attributed to secret societies, the typical eyes and flaky skin characteristic of reptiles) in all kinds of media texts (see Stæhr 2014).

Contrary to the popular opinion that evolved in the spirit of moral panic, many researchers are of the opinion that the expansion of conspiracy theories into online communication does not reflect a conspiracy panic taking hold of the masses, nor even an existence of beliefs in conspiracies considerably stronger than in earlier times (Fenster 2008, 245; Weimann 2003, 348–349; van Prooijen, Douglas 2018, 4). The majority of visitors of conspiracy websites are characterised by a half-cynical, half-serious attitude, both to the official versions of the events affecting communal life as well as to the conspiracy theories (Knight 2002, 6). Online communities that mediate conspiracy theories often do not offer one coherent explanation of the events, while outlining several alternative versions of the same events is fairly widespread (Knight 2008, 186). Contemporary conspiracy culture invites one to draw one's own conclusions and to doubt everything, including evidence and explanations offered by other conspiracy theorists (Knight 2008, 192). Visiting websites proposing conspiracy theories is, among other things, motivated by the component of entertainment (Johnson 2018), occasionally these pages lead their visitors to join open-ended, self-perpetuating interpretation games that make it possible to surf through various images, videos and diagrams and construct different versions of the conspiracy (Soukup 2008, 20). It is important to note that interactive conspiracy sites that bring together many users blend imaginative and humorous descriptions of conspiracies with explanations expressing sincere concern and fear of conspiracies. Thus, memes ridiculing conspiracy theories and their creators (Piata 2016) and satirical parodies (Bessi et al. 2015a) may become components in so-called serious stories pointing at omnipotent conspiracies (Stano 2020), and the other way round. In summary, navigators in conspiracy webs will find it difficult to "distinguish fact from fiction; real evidence from false evidence and, ultimately, to discover the real truth underneath the pile of interpretations and Babylonian language games" (Aupers 2012, 27). So, they scan the bits of information they come across (including those deriving from the so-called official information sphere) through a lens of permanent scepticism and trust the content that corroborates their own intuition or gut feeling.

On the role of conspiracy theories in the rhetoric of radicalising social media groups

On the other hand, several studies have brought forward the idea that conspiracy theories contribute to the introversion of social media groups concentrating around extremist world views and to the radicalisation of the ideas prevailing there (Askanius, Mylonas 2015; Bessi et al. 2015a, 2016; Lewandowsky et al. 2017; Madisson, Ventsel 2016a; Sunstein, Vermeule 2009; Singer, Brooking 2018) and can even lead to concrete acts of violence. These are mostly connected with alt-right "lone wolves" who have become radicalised in web communities and find an expression in conspiracy theories for translating their vague feeling of social oppression and injustice into the language of concrete aims (Griffin 2003, 47; Madisson 2016b, 190). Anders Behring Breivik, who was influenced by Eurabian conspiracy theories (see Fekete 2012; Turner-Graham 2014), and Brenton Tarrant, who in turn was inspired by Breivik's conspiracy theory (Önnerfors 2019), serve as notorious examples of such radicalisation. This radicalisation pattern also characterised Edgar Maddison Welch who made an armed rush into Comet Ping Pong pizzeria to put an end to a conspiracy of Satanist human traffickers and paedophiles (see Bergmann 2018; Johnson 2018; Singer, Brooking 2018).

Studies point out that social media users who actively follow conspiracy threads tend to be of the erroneous opinion that belief in conspiracies is widespread in society (Lewandowsky et al. 2017, 362). Also, being present in such an information space will considerably strengthen antagonistic attitudes towards official explanations (e.g. information obtained from scientists or government institutions) (Einstein, Glick 2015; Jolley, Douglas 2013; Lewandowsky et al. 2013; Madisson 2016a; Howard 2013). Several studies have found that different populist or even extremist movements have been systematically spreading conspiracy theory threads on social media in order to strengthen the victim mentality mobilising the audience and the oppositional attitudes to the political elite and mainstream media (Berger 2016; Bergmann 2018; Kasekamp et al. 2019; Krasodomski-Jones 2019). The problem of communities mediating conspiracy theories that facilitate the formation of echo chambers and social polarisation has been lately recognised also by social media platforms, as

YouTube (Murphy 2018) and Twitter (Wong 2018a) have made announcements regarding taking specific means to counter this.

Conspiracy theories as part of strategic communication

Several studies have treated the spreading and/or amplifying of conspiracy theories on social media as part of strategic communication. Due to their attention-grabbing effect caused by their intriguing and sensational nature, conspiracy theories make it possible to draw valuable social media traffic to accounts representing a certain agenda; for instance, it has been suggested that it this reason that Donald Trump's presidential campaign team (Singer, Brooking 2018; Johnson 2018; Krasodomski-Jones 2019) and accounts connected with the Kremlin troll network (Broniatowski et al. 2018; Kragh, Åsberg 2017; Marwick, Lewis 2017) have been spreading anti-vaccination conspiracy theories. It has been pointed out that both accounts connected with the Kremlin and with Trump disseminate content created by Alex Jones, one of the most popular and influential conspiracy theorists (Benkler et al. 2018; Marwick, Lewis 2017). Connections with Jones's strong personal brand and the image of Infowars as a radical anti-elitist media platform make it possible for their messages to gain credibility in the eyes of the audience segment who doubt the so-called official explanations. Also, studies have pointed out that Russia continuously spreads anti-Western conspiracy theories with the help of sock puppets[1] and bots that allow them to sow distrust of other national governments and media into their audiences and magnify the pre-existing rifts in societies (Pomerantsev, Weiss 2014; Flaherty, Roselle 2018; Jantunen 2018). Both Infowars and the Russian media channels Sputnik and RT, which serve the aims of Russia's information influencing, suggest that their audiences themselves should obtain evidence of conspiracies in which Western regimes are engaged from the content mediated by Wikileaks and other leaking sites (Johnson 2018; Yablokov 2015). Such sources are attractive to conspiracy-interested audiences as they are secret and offer abundant informational raw material, as it were, that can be given a meaningful shape by placing it into a framework of conspiracy theories (Jantunen 2018, 121).

Scholars of strategic communication have noted that conspiracy theories are also being used in order to exhaust and disorient the audience or to create an information fog that was briefly discussed in the subchapter "Information conflicts and strategic narratives". Information fog is an influencing technique in which the interpreter is deliberately fed narratives that are in conflict with one another, while the aim of the activity is to generate general distrust and the feeling that it is virtually impossible to differentiate between right and wrong (Nissen 2015, 11). Dissemination of conspiracy theories that concern the same event and in principle exclude one another has been noticed, for instance, in Russia's strategic communication (Flaherty, Roselle 2018; Ventsel et al. 2019; Yablokov 2015). An explosive spread of conspiracy narratives creating such information fog could be observed after the revelation of Sergei and Yulia

Skripal's poisoning case in 2018 (Livingston, Nassetta 2018). A secret network of Russophobes, the British Secret Service, Georgia, Ukraine, Sweden and the US were pointed at as responsible for the event; in addition, a theory was circulated that there had been no poisoning and the event had simply been staged in order to damage Russia's reputation. When using information fog it is important to sketch emphatically the contradictions between different accounts and to repeat stories that are in conflict with each other, thus the audience will remain clueless while aware that something suspicious is going on and it is worthwhile being extremely sceptical about any reports on the topic (Ventsel et al. 2019). In such conditions, interpreters tend to proceed from the affective recognition, or the so-called collective gut feeling, shaped in the echo chambers of social media that connects unpleasant events and developments with a criminal force (see Marmura 2014).

As was pointed out previously, this book first and foremost treats conspiracy theories in the framework of strategic communication. A large part of the battle for the "hearts and minds" of the audience is to a greater or lesser degree connected with different aspects of identity creation. In the following subchapter we concentrate on the identity-creation functions of conspiracy theories that can be used in order to achieve strategic aims.

The functions of identity creation in conspiracy theories

It was pointed out in the subchapter "Information conflicts and information warfare" that influencing activities focused on the cognitive level of the contemporary information war are usually based on the inclusion and exclusion logic of identity creation. For the disseminators of strategic conspiracy theories, the constructing of conflict situations in which a narrative that has been shaped simultaneously attempts to offer possible solutions to conflict is of fundamental importance. Such a conflict or problem is always constructed in the sense of being dependent on the particular articulation processes. Following the theory of Ernesto Laclau and Chantal Mouffe, identity discourse is understood here as an outcome of the practice of articulation, which establishes a relation among elements in such a way that the identity of elements is modified as a result of the articulation (Laclau, Mouffe 1985). In the context of social media, the contestation of dominant discourses and identity creation is expressed via accepted as well as unaccepted (misinformation, trolling, etc.) actions, and it is predominantly associated with the demand for recognition of identification of participants in communication (Dahlberg 2011, 861; Dahlgren 2006). It is important to note that the field of application of the concept of discourse is not only limited to writing or speech, but that it refers to any system of elements where *relations* play a constitutive role.

Generally speaking, a conspiracy theory has been defined as an articulation of an unpleasant event as being the result of a conspiracy. "Conspiracy theory is a proposed explanation of some historical event (or events) in terms of the significant casual agency of relatively small group of persons – conspirators – acting in secret" (Keeley 1999, 116). These interpretative frames are often in conflict with other ways of modelling the world. Conspiracy theories have become an important device for the re-allocation of power between different actors and an efficient element in socio-political strategies (Yablokov 2015). This means that conspiracy theories play a significant role in the articulation and legitimisation of identities (Madisson 2016a). Conspiracy theories do not only give explanations to *why* we are beset by tragic misfortunes, but also sketch (of course, with varying degrees of explicitness) the level that explains *how the event occurred and how it affects us*, i.e. the particular time-space of actions, the relationship of the conspirators with the existing institutions and the functioning principles of their various manipulation techniques, etc. (Madisson 2014; see Armstrong 2009).

In the following we present the dominants of identity creation in the conspiracy-theoretical discourse and its main socio-communicative functions. The dominant may be defined as the focusing component of a meaningful semiotic unity: it rules, determines and transforms the remaining components. It is the dominant which guarantees the integrity of the structure (Jakobson 1971a, 82). If we analyse a conspiracy theory as a semiotic unit, we shall be able to distinguish a dominant that will determine the general meaning of the conspiracy theory and the function it fulfils.

Symbolic function of conspiracy theories of identity creation

As mentioned above, any formation of social identities necessarily involves inclusion/exclusion relations and "associated discursive contestation, where discourse is understood as a contingent and partial fixation of meaning that constitutes and organizes social relations (including identities, objects, and practices)" (Dahlberg 2011, 861). The communication of conspiracy theorists is characterised by strongly polarised identity creation in which an antagonistic opposition of "us" and "them" serves as an important dominant. The articulation of such an identity based on an antagonistic opposition and the belief in its relevance certainly vary, but this is a typical opposition characteristic of various conspiracy theories (Ventsel 2016b). The information field of conspiracy theories is usually united by the conviction that the greater part of contemporary social processes are an immediate result of a malicious conspiracy (Madisson 2014) and that the world is being conquered by an avaricious and corrupt elite (in most interpretations also perceived as implicitly malevolent) that operates in secrecy. Its aim is to submit the whole world to its global authoritarian regime. According to the English historian and political scientist Roger Griffin conspiracy theorists consider the cultural homogenisation, globalising economy and mass migration that concern the whole world to be an indicator of the success and omnipresence of such conspiracy. In connection with this, not only passive complaints about the decadence of the prevailing world order are uttered, but often also ideas for a radical reform of the world system are articulated (Griffin 2002, 49).

Conspiracy theories spreading today combine classic plot types of conspiracy theories and antagonists: freemasons, political elites of any country, Jews, Catholics, aliens. Antagonists may vary from politically extremist explanations to pseudoscientific or spiritual fragments (Barkun 2003, 182–184). The explosive growth of the accessibility and dissemination of information brought about by hypermedia has only made the spectrum more varied (Dean 2002, 97–98; Fenster 2008, 160–161). History is not a chaotic process: there is no accident, fate or contingency in history. In the words of the French sociologist Julien Giry and Turkish historian Doğan Gürpınar, if everything has a unique cause, everything is reducible to conspiracy theories and consequently some totally contradictory situations must be seen as different manifestations of the (same) conspiracy. The *symbolic* function of conspiracy theories suggests an apparently coherent historical narration (Giry, Gürpına 2020) that constitutes the world as two sides in a permanent conflict situation. Thus, one of the main functions of conspiracy theories overlaps with a function of strategic narratives – to offer an organising and meaningful narrative to the contingency of history.

Conspiracy theories as mobilisers of communities

Another important function characteristic of the world models of conspiracy theories is the mobilising function. Conspiracy theories reduce various negative social developments and misfortunes to the active agency of Evil. Evil can and should be fought against, either by revealing its minions or neutralising it in another way. Who embodies the function of Evil is, in principle, contingent and depends on the socio-political situation (Madisson 2014). According to Svetlana Boym, the dedicated creators of conspiracy theories have a heightened sense of mission and have been expelled to subcultures unknown to the general public, much like the conspirers themselves, yet they nevertheless attempt to thwart the schemes of the conspirators (1999, 7). As conspiracy theories point out a singular enemy responsible for everything evil, they otherwise fulfil a function of *mobilisation*: they offer a means of defence to those who feel themselves to be harmed (Giry, Gürpına 2020). What is important at this point is the sociological observation that conspiracy theories are especially likely to be endorsed by those who are convinced that their group is not valued or acknowledged enough by others (Golec de Zavala et al. 2009; van Prooijen, Douglas 2018). Such feeling is linked to an increased sensitivity to threats (Cichocka 2016; Golec de Zavala et al. 2016).

In this context, we can conceptualise the conspiracy theory as a process of meaning-making whose objective is "the transformation of a social relation which constructs a subject in a relationship of subordination" (Laclau, Mouffe 1985, 153; see also Laclau 1990, 172; Marchart 2007, Ch. 2), and the conflict contained in conspiracy theories is directly presented as being of public consequence (Howarth, Glynos 2007, 115). *Professional* conspiracy theorists or *political entrepreneurs* in conspiracy theories (Campion-Vincent 2015;

Giry 2015), are likely to see conspiracy theories as a way to subvert the political field and its agenda directly or indirectly. In other words, conspiracy theorists compete with the established political elites by mobilising some resources outside of the traditional political field that they can use within it (Giry, Gürpına 2020).

Conspiracy theories as sources of communion cohesion

In connection with identity formation, the discourse of conspiracy theories displays its specific function *confirming* social ties. The semantic value of information transmitted by conspiracy theories is relatively minimal. Even if there should be new bits of information (new antagonist and new events), they will be fitted into an already existing interpretation framework that is directed by an understanding that behind all misdeeds and misfortunes lurks the plotting of one and the same malevolent group operating in secrecy. There is, in principle, no major difference if the main force behind the plot is supported by Jews; black, Asian and minority ethnic (BAME) people; or radical Islamists, as they are all in the service of the Big Evil – American financial elites. However, this lack of new semantic value in conspiracy theories is compensated for by their strong potential for creating communal ties that is particularly evident in social media communication.

Many studies approaching the contemporary public information and discussion culture have noted that information practices dominating in social media are characterised by acceleration, saturation and a strong affective loadedness. An exponentially growing number of texts are converging in peoples' news streams and magnifying a feeling of connectedness and involvement, and the shared experiencing of texts has become an ever more important parameter in gaining users' attention (see Andrejevic 2013; Grusin 2010; Harsin 2014, 2015; Miller 2008; Prøitz 2017). Such communication is characterised by quick and brief text creation that to a great extent is based on repetition and amplifying shared emotions; and does not presuppose thorough discussions and logical argumentation. We treat such communication by disseminators of conspiracy theorists in the framework of the phatic function of language suggested by the linguist and semiotician Roman Jakobson (1976).

According to Jakobson, the predominance of the phatic function in communication may be expressed in a lavish exchange of ritual formulas and whole dialogues whose only aim is to maintain communication. The phatic function is directed at the contact, "a physical channel and psychological connection between the addresser and the addressee, enabling both of them to enter and stay in communication" (Jakobson 1976, 113). Jakobson was mostly engaged with examples from linguistics. At the same time he was of the opinion that "this pragmatic approach to language must lead *mutatis mutandis* to an analogous study of the other semiotic systems: with which of these or other functions are they endowed, in what combinations and in what hierarchical order?" (Jakobson 1971b, 703). Thus examples of communication with a phatic dominant can also include audio-visual texts used by conspiracy theorists, whose information value has become lost, but which serve to maintain the feeling of communion: secret signs, formulas that have lost their meaning, number combinations, acronyms or fragments of particular texts (e.g. song lyrics, aphorisms, phrases exchanged in an offline-context and marking group belonging, etc., known to insiders). These kind of signals, phatic posts and other small, micro-symbols indicate the recognition of one's interlocutor's presence and validation of them as a potential communicative partner (Radovanovic, Ragnedda 2012, 12). To a broader audience, the messages of conspiracy theorists thus often seem incoherent, while the target group familiar with particular codes is able to exchange private messages via comparatively public channels, e.g. social media environments, blogs, newspapers' comments sections, etc. (Siibak 2012; see also Madisson, Ventsel 2018).

In such communication the meaning of words is nearly irrelevant. The expressions are rather used in the function of confirming social ties, which can be expressed in, e.g., establishing an intimate atmosphere conducive of social connection. The information exchanged in the course of phatic communication is indexical rather than referential, it reflects the (in)acceptance of the communication partner and attributes a certain status to them (Laver 1975, 336). Thus, the above-mentioned private signs of conspiracy theorists have turned into phatic signs in the course of being used. In many cases, phatic communication presumes recognition, intimacy and sociability from the participants, that constitute founding blocks of communions. On the other hand, the connection itself becomes more significant, the words more redundant (Miller 2008, 395).

In summary, the figure of the conspirator makes it possible for conspiracy theorists to give explanations to social contradictions and deviations from (ideal) social life as well as create a vision of a world whose meaning is coherent. At the same time, conspiracy theories allow for mobilising the communion and shape its self-image. A successful strategy should be able to communicate these functions effectively to an audience.

The semiotic approach to conspiracy narratives

This chapter concentrates on mapping various academic studies of conspiracy theories. We present an original semiotic approach to conspiracy theories that is based on the logic of discrete and non-discrete meaning-making, united by the notion of the code text, that derives from semiotics of culture. The code text allows us to explain the specific tendencies of meaning-making that dominate in conspiracy theories.

Studying the mode of modelling conspiracy theories from the point of view of culture research

From the semiotic perspective, it is noteworthy that although a conspiracy theory can appear in different contexts and be transmitted via various channels, it nevertheless remains recognisable as a conspiracy theory – as a text sustaining specific relations of meaning. The spectrum of conspiracy theories is extremely broad. They are mediated by media of various kinds, for example verbal speech, the printed word, diverse pictorial means of expression (drawings, diagrams, photos), videos, and contemporary interactive and hybrid textual compositions combining all the above. Existing research on conspiracy theories has thus considered them to be characteristic of political rhetoric, especially its populist forms (Pipes 1999; Bergmann 2018; Yablokov 2018), but conspiracy theories are also seen as a *lingua franca* of alternative and counter cultures (Knight 2002; Vincent 2006), and a sustaining structure of popular psychology texts, for example self-help books that encourage people to quit a life designed by someone else and finally become themselves (Melley 2002). Other aspects that researchers have focused on are vernacular conspiracy theories (see Campion-Vincent 2005; Astapova 2017) and artistic texts mediating conspiracy theories – films (Donovan 2011) and novels (Wisnicki 2007).

Also, other qualitative approaches have treated conspiracy theories as a particular type of discourse emerging in various contexts or a mode of modelling creating specific connections. Our emphases are shared by research from the fields of cultural studies and critical theory, with work by Jack Bratich (2004, 2008), Clare Birchall (2006), Mark Fenster (2008) and Dean Ballinger (2011) as prominent examples. All these studies see popular media as one of the key factors in contemporary conspiracy culture and highlight the fact that in the past decades conspiracy theories have become commodified and turned into a constituent part of mass media on course to becoming increasingly more like infotainment. Thus, they should not be attributed to peripheral subcultures and "losers" only.[2] Similarly, with several studies of conspiracy cultures conducted within culture research (Birchall 2006; Aupers 2012; Fenster 2008) we admit that in principle conspiracies are possible (there are separate paragraphs concerning these in criminal law, for instance regarding seizing power or organised criminal activities) and history has witnessed conspiracies (e.g. the events revealed in the Watergate affair in 1972, the planning of Operation Northwoods in 1962). In a sense, the deliberate dissemination of disinformation based on conspiracy theories that occurs on social media is also a conspiracy being brought to life through conspiracy theories that in a conscious, hidden and biased manner influence the masses' perception of the situation. Still, it should be underscored that in open societies, the occurrence of large-scale deliberate conspiracies potentially harmful to many citizens, such as the programme of eradication of the white race, deliberate spreading of disease by poisonous vaccines and unleashing of infections etc., is very unlikely and it is difficult to hide events such as these from the public for a significant length of time.

For studies focusing on the conspiracy discourse, the references and correspondence to reality of particular versions of conspiracy theories are not particularly relevant. Rather, the focus is on the rhetorical and argumentative lines repeating in conspiracy theories that create an aura of secrecy, articulate the positions of the oppressors and the oppressed (Birchall 2006; Leone 2017) and fix a so-called contagious pattern of associations that directs the interpreters towards discovering ever new conspiracy layers (Fenster 2008; Madisson 2016b). The works of Bratich and Birchall (see also Dean 2002; Fiske 1994) concentrate on the counterhegemonic potentiality of conspiracy discourse. Namely, they have been clarifying the situations in which the interpretative framework of conspiracy theories cultivates critical attitudes towards traditional authorities and their canons of objectivity. Bratich (2008, 187) and Birchall (2006, 62) point out that conspiracy theories provide a language for articulating and highlighting the problem of social, political and economic inequalities. This book draws on the comments referenced above first and foremost in cases in which we analyse the vernacular discourse of knowledge that opposes the mainstream. However, our aim is to demonstrate the plurality of functions of conspiracy theories, among others also its applicability as a strategic tool of the dominant regime.

Dean Ballinger's doctoral dissertation (Ballinger 2011) focuses on the specificity of the digital conspiracy discourse (see also Knight 2008; Soukup 2008) and the identity creation dominants of online conspiracy theorists. Ballinger explains how online conspiracy theorists are mapping their conspiracy investigation by relying on the discourse of cyber democracy. He contends that conspiracy theorists understand mainstream media as a sphere of conspiratorial propaganda, disinformation and/or mind control (Ballinger 2011, 65). Ballinger's analysis demonstrates how the positive self-image of a radical citizen journalist allows the placement of conspiracy theorists "outside the traditional structures of mainstream media and accentuate the radical and romantic impulses that are innate to the conspiracist mindset [...]" (Ballinger 2011, 73). Our approach relies on Ballinger's insights about the potential of conspiracy theories in creating a positive self-description of their disseminators. We also draw on his remarks on the adaptation of conspiracy theories to web discourse, but also develop this direction of research further, for Ballinger's dissertation appeared at the start of the present decade and did not cover the affordances of social media and tendencies in communication.

The monograph by Mark Fenster (2008) thoroughly discusses the manifestation of conspiracy theory as a specific way of modelling in political rhetoric as well as in various fictional texts. Fenster weaves into his thorough treatment works by several classics of semiotics, e.g. Roland Barthes, Algirdas J. Greimas and Joseph Courtés, Charles Sanders Peirce etc. Similarly to us, Fenster conceptualises the peculiarities of the interpretive practices of conspiracy theories. Drawing on Umberto Eco's (1990) framework of hermetic semiosis he aptly explains the tendency of conspiracy theorists "to seize and fetishize individual signs in order to place them within vast interpretive structures" (Fenster 2008, 13). The conspiracy theorists' interpretation processes are directed by the presumption that there exist extremely significant missing links or compromising traces that prove the existence of the conspiracy itself. Whenever they discover a piece of such "evidence", an enthusiastic search for analogous evidence is launched, in the course of which they carefully examine media content in order to find interpretative keys that would disclose their hidden meanings to the wider audience. Conspiracy theorists may treat various elements of public media discourse, e.g. illustrations, number-combinations, slips of the tongue etc. as anchors that enable them to fix the chain of analogies (Leone et al. 2020).

The explanations Fenster gives to the conspiracy theory as a text type are significant from the point of view of this book as well (also see Birchall 2006; Butter 2014). According to Fenster, the interpretation of some events as part of a conspiracy requires a temporal-causal chain, while it is irrelevant whether the event influenced by the conspirators is discovered among past or future experiences. Presuming that a key role in social events is played by the activities of conspirators, interpreters keep actively looking for evidence of the conspiracy. A particular event will become significant if the interpreters can connect it with earlier and later conspiracy acts in a broader conspiracy narrative (Fenster 2008, 100–106). In developing our framework, we rely on Fenster's remarks on the central role of temporal-causal or discrete connections in organising conspiracy representations, but we offer a model that explains the associative or non-discrete organising components of conspiracy theories. To be more precise, we are offering a model based on the framework of the code text that explains the co-functioning of two different dominants in text creation. In addition to this, our approach gives new insights into explaining the meaning potentials of conspiracy narratives in the context of strategic communication.

The model of meaning-making on the basis of the code text of conspiracy theories

In our earlier work we have been developing a cultural semiotic model (see Madisson 2014; Madisson 2016b; Ventsel 2016a) that makes it possible to explicate the invariant mechanisms of meaning-making that are common to all conspiracy narratives. Conspiracy narratives are made specific by their particularly strong modelling capacity that allows them easily to embrace in their explanations events from different points of time and space and weave into a synthetic whole symbols and sources that seem totally incompatible at first sight. Apparently, such an enormous modelling capacity is a reason why conspiracy theories have become especially valued in these contemporary times of information overload – they offer a shortcut to strong meanings that can be easily perceived. Conspiracy theories speak of secret plots, hiding, villains and conspiration patterns connecting various tragic events. Although such components are repeated from one conspiracy theory to another and are thus already familiar to the interpreters, they can still catch attention if intriguing hints pertinent to the moment are newly woven into them. Earlier we have been employing the semiotic model of conspiracy theories first and foremost in analysing far-right online communication and identity creation (Madisson, Ventsel 2016a, 2016b, 2018), but in this book we wish to show its broader potential in disseminating various strategic messages and nudging the context necessary for directing the readers' interpretative paths.

It seems expedient to conceptualise conspiracy theories proceeding from the frame of the code text by Juri Lotman (1988), so it is possible to give an explanation to the peculiar meaning-making of conspiracy narratives that unites both an associative as well as a verbal-discrete component. Lotman has defined the code text as a textual system that originates from the collective memory of a particular community. He describes it as a specific meaning-making template or an interlink that, instead of being an abstract collection of rules for constructing a text, is a textual system with a rigid syntactic order. The different signs of a code text can be divided into various sub-structures, but despite this the code text remains unambiguous "for itself": "from the standpoint of its own level, the sign is something invested not only with a unity of expression but also with a unity of content" (Lotman 1988b, 35; see Madisson 2014, 292; Madisson 2016a, 201). A conspiracy theory behaves like a code text that tells the story about the Evil lurking behind particular events, while its constituent parts, such as the articulation of the specificity of the enemy, the connections of particular evidence of conspiracy with certain events, outlines of the victims, etc., can embrace various paradigms (Madisson 2014, 293). The universal message or code text of conspiracy theory is: this (whatever unpleasant event) is a conspiracy, i.e. the realisation of a malevolent plot of a covert grouping (Madisson 2014, 294). This set of relations is highly adaptive and can be filled with situation-specific content (Madisson 2014, 294; Melley 2002, 59).

Discrete and non-discrete logic of code-textual meaning-making

It is important to note that the code-text of conspiracy theories involves both discrete as well as non-discrete principle of signification. The former is related to the fact that the articulation of relations of cause and effect, chronology and logic is an important organising core in conspiracy narratives (Madisson 2014, 290). It can even be claimed that the code text of conspiracy theories favours over-deterministic models of causation that do not leave space for fortuitous chance and coincidence, but view all socially meaningful events as connected to one another by a conspiracy (Madisson 2014, 297). In addition to outlining strict relations of cause and effect, discrete logic also is concerned with representing a complex conspiracy system. Narratives speaking of wide-ranging and long-lasting conspiracies, i.e. super conspiracies (e.g. NWO), outline a hierarchical and complex conspiracy pyramid that manipulates different aspects of communal life (see Madisson 2016). For instance, there is a relatively widespread idea that, in order to establish their absolute power and hinder all critical thought and resistance, sub-branches of the conspiracy system have, on the one hand, been specialising in influencing the information sphere, which means they have infiltrated the education system starting with kindergartens up to universities and that they control the media. On the other hand, conspirators are active in the physical weakening of the population, which is why they spread diseases, produce poisonous vaccines, contaminate food, cause natural disasters, etc.

A special characteristic of the code text of conspiracy theory is that the sketching of discrete meaning relations is always submitted to non-discrete logic of signification that is associative and based on analogies. All in all, the non-discrete modelling that serves as the basis of conspiracy theories means that interpreters identify signs of conspiracies in the case of a particular event or piece of information. It is an interpretative tendency that we defined as hermetic semiosis in the previous subchapter, following Eco and Fenster. In narratives talking about systemic conspiracies drawing parallels and seeing patterns serves as an important principle of creating connections. Still, it is important to notice that it is not a metaphoric relation of sameness, but that conspiracy theories actually presume that the same forces are behind all unpleasant events, that keep leaving similar traces of their activities.

Shaping of meaning relations in conspiracy theories is organised by the idea of large-scale concealment and a malevolent group as a force triggering all kinds of change, which already exists in the memory of the interpretative community. A contemporary example of interpretative community could be social media groups that are gathering around common thematic and ideological foci, in which spokespersons, shared values and communication norms, as well as a specific discursive code become established. In Eco's terms, they develop a shared base vocabulary in the course of continuous communication, we can recognise the rhetorical and stylistic codes of insiders and they also form a common memory repertoire that embraces typical agents and standard scripts connected with these (see the subchapter "The Model Reader and the image of the audience"). Interpretative communities sharing conspiracy theories develop a permutation of so-called typical elements and key figures of conspiracy explanations which are syncretically combined when suspicious events occur (Barkun 2003, 183; Madisson 2016a, 196). For instance, such phrases as *Deep state, NWO, Cultural Marxists, ZOG, The Bilderberg Group* often serve as triggers that unleash specific conspiracy scenarios in the interpretative community's communal memory and the association chains connected with these. To summarise the above, it can be concluded that the code text based meaning-making of conspiracy theories is somewhat redundant – the interpretative community generates messages whose main content (that all tragic developments are connected with a conspiracy in one way or another) is known to them already. The main aim of such messages is rather the reduction of the unknown to known plots and the guarantee of cohesion of the community and a positive feedback loop, so that it largely fulfils the phatic function that is mobilising the community. One important aspect of conspiracy communication is that not only the information fragments and "events that are perceived as a result of conspiracy become more meaningful but also the conspiracy itself will become more confirmed and significant because of frequent interpretations" (Madisson 2016a, 205).

Another important aspect of the non-discrete logic of conspiracy narratives is binary modelling of the world, as there is a tendency to divide it into agents of Good and Evil. The more terrible the consequences of any particular event are, the more brutal and inhuman must be the conspirators who intentionally caused it. It should be emphasised that conspiracy narratives represent conspirators as active agents with clear purpose – they do not damage the well-being of large groups of people by chance or unintentionally, but as a result of deliberate and extremely purposeful action. Lotman has pointed out that binary thinking does not even consider the relative equality of the concerned parties. Even if acknowledging such equality may not mean admitting the opponent's right to the truth, it would at least mean admitting its right to existence (Lotman 2007, 26). As a rule, conspiracy theories sketch a conflict in which the opponent is perceived as corrupt and immoral so that entering a dialogue or reaching a compromise with them is in principle excluded. Thus, the logic of conspiracy theories sees the elimination of the conspiracy (and at times also the conspirators) as the only positive solution. Representing such an ultimately corrupt opposing force also provides a perfect background for positive self-descriptions or self-positioning as the moral victim who is hated by an immensely powerful enemy that operates in secrecy. The strategy of constructing conflict proceeding from binary modelling will be treated in more detail in the following part of the book.

Presuming the immensely powerful will or, to be more exact, the immanent malevolence that causes an insolvable conflict between the conspirators and those that revealed it, is the main centre of the code text of conspiracy theories that subsumes to itself the discrete logic of signification. In other words, the code text of conspiracy theories generates modelling that is based on a specific causality that can be reduced to intentionality. Being convinced of the sinister will of conspirators, functions as a powerful principle and is perceived as the driving force of history taken as a whole (Fenster 2008, 103; Hofstadter 1967, 29). As demonstrated above, this does not mean that conspiracy theories neglect the logic of the physical, historical and social causalities that are related with particular events. Quite the opposite – the conditions in which a particular event happened are often depicted in an incredibly detailed way. Madisson suggests that the reason why conspirators are perceived as extremely threatening is that interpreters presume that they have the capacity to manipulate all kinds of causality for serving their evil intentions, and they hide it in so advanced a way that most people would never notice it. Thus, conspiracy narrative "acknowledges the diversity of various phenomena/relations but, at the same time, it assumes that different events are motivated by evil as the ultimate and all-embracing cause. As various dimensions of reality are perceived as parts of the same system of evil, the attributes that are essential for distinguishing such structures are vague" (Madisson 2016a, 202).

This chapter demonstrated the specific creation of connections of conspiracy theories and the main emphases emerging in studying them proceeding from culture research and semiotics. All in all, it can be noted that the code text resulting from the communal memory of the conspiracy theory's interpretative community inspires the creation of conspiracy narratives that include explanations as to *how*, as well as *why*, tragic events and developments have occurred. The following chapters will show how the specific meaning creation in conspiracy theories can be employed in strategic communication in order to articulate and amplify particular conflicts.

Notes

1 In the context of information influence activities, Thomas Elkjær Nissen explains a sock puppet as, "a fake identity created to promote someone or something through blogs, wikis, forums or social networking sites such as Facebook or Twitter. Sock puppets are often created to improve the status of some entity or to promote a particular viewpoint that is expected to be helpful to that entity." (Nissen 2015: 87).
2 Joseph E. Uscinski and Joseph M. Parent are famous for the statement that conspiracy theories tend to resonate when groups are suffering from loss, weakness or disunity (see Uscinski, Parent 2014).

Part II

Semiotic analysis of strategic Soros-themed conspiracy narratives

3 Strategic Soros-themed conspiracy narratives in politics, marketing and alternative knowledge

The first part of the book treated the semiotic conflict from the point of view of the strategic narrative and proposed a semiotic discussion of the conspiracy narrative. The second part points at concrete textual devices through which conflicts and participants in conflicts – their protagonists and antagonists – can be shaped in strategic conspiracy narratives seen as special cases of the strategic narrative. In our opinion, the nature of the audiences forming around conspiracy narratives mostly depends on the specificity of modelling the conflict and its prevailing meaning-making mechanisms. In the first half of this chapter we complement the model of the conspiracy narrative with treating *the topic* (Eco 2005). This will enable us to understand better how the code-textual meaning-making, that serves as the basis of conspiracy narratives, is directed by conflict as the specific centre of organising interpretations. In the second half of the chapter, we provide examples of conspiracy narratives from the fields of politics, alternative knowledge and marketing, and analyse how the character of conflict constitutes the relationships between the characters and events featuring in them.

Strategic construction of conflict in conspiracy narrative

One of the main functions of the strategic narrative is to offer the audience a frame for structuring the past, present and future of conflicts (Nissen 2015, 45). Such a set of relations will lead the audience towards various snippets of text or narrative, which is why the shapers of strategic narratives have to take into account the existing narratives and other factors directing the interpretative atmosphere (see subchapter "The Model Reader and the image of the audience"). In the context of researching social media communication it appears important that, in the model offered by Eco, there is no assumption that the interpretative process should go through all the stages in a particular order. Interpretation may also occur as an explosion or in long "leaps". The reader has a certain hypothesis that brings forth an interpretative explosion (Eco 2005, 75). The shaper of the strategic narrative first has to create the hypothesis in the reader.

It is conflict constructed as the centre of the code text of conspiracy narratives that has the function of triggering the reader's interpretation hypothesis. As was pointed out at the end of the previous chapter, the code text of conspiracy narratives establishes the existence of a network of malicious conspirators. Conspiracy narratives represent enormously influential actors who in their actions proceed from the *Evil* or amorality that is in their nature. Naturally, the mode of articulating such motifs varies from one conspiracy narrative to another, but predominantly they all contain an implicit vision of conspirators aiming to subdue the people in the world to their own will to as great an extent as possible. In the context of strategic communication, it becomes important how the conflict has been constructed in creating the Model Reader and how it functions in meaning-making.

Conflict as the topic

From the perspective of meaning-making conflict functions as the centre – the topic – of the conspiracy narrative. Determining such a topic is a cooperative (pragmatic) step that directs the reader towards differentiating between the semantic properties of the text (Eco 2005, 108–109). In this sense, the topic differs from the fabula that represents the events of a tale as a chronological and causal sequence and simultaneously constitutes a part of the text's message. According to Eco (2005, 95), the fabula is connected with the semantic structure of the tale, while the topic can first and foremost be treated as a pragmatic instrument that supports the reader's interpretation process. Thus, the topic need not necessarily have an explicit textual expression, but the interpreter creates it in the process of his or her reception of the text as a direction leading his or her path of interpretation. Such a direction that leads the process of interpretation is formed in the interplay of the text and the cultural competence of the reader interpreting it; thus, it need not always be a conscious and calculated choice on part of the interpreter. One of the main functions of the topic is delimiting or, as it were, disciplining the interpretation process, but it also functions as a guide of smaller text parts and discursive structures (Eco 2005, 95), as the latter "need to be actualised in the light of the hypothesis made regarding the topic or the topics" (Eco 2005, 94). It is important to stress the dynamic, relational nature of the topic as there are "sentence topics and discourse topics that disappear when there is a transition to the abstraction of the text's 'dominat theme'" (Eco 2005, 95).

For strategic communication to be successful, the narrative's author has to create a Model Reader whose textual devices push the interpreter towards creating a direction or hypothesis supporting the intentions of the actor/author. Treating conflicts as a topic helps us explain how to direct strategically the code-textual meaning-making that serves as the basis of conspiracy narratives or how such a direction or hypothesis can be created in the interpreter. In addition to a fundamental conflict, conspiracy narratives also contain a series of other conflicts of more local importance – their subtopics. Thus, the conflict of the global NWO conspiracy narrative is formed of a sequence of subconflicts the shaping of which largely depends on the socio-cultural background where they are articulated. These subconflicts can be reconstructed on the basis of a rhetorical-stylistic code in which, e.g., Soros's Jewish heritage makes it possible to employ ethnic stereotypes in representing the conflict; at the same time, the conflict can be encoded on the basis of an ideological code that emphasises Soros's actions as an initiator of projects that advocate a liberal world view.

Thus one of the main tasks of semiotic analysis of strategic communication is to find out how the Model Reader is being led towards reconstructing the topic, for it is largely on the basis of the topic that an interpreter either amplifies some semantic properties of existing units of meaning or, to the contrary, tones them down. In either case the level of interpretative cohesion is established in the course of such action. Below, we differentiate between two types of constructing conflicts – an antithetical and an agonistic one. These direct different aspects of forming the narrative and help interpreters create coherence, while the disseminators have to take them into account in the course of their communicative action.

Antithetical and agonistic modelling of conflict

As we pointed out in the subchapter "The ontology of the semiotic conflict", from the perspective of semiotics the specificity of conflict is determined by the nature of the boundary or translation mechanism. The boundary is the most important functional and structural position of semiotic space that determines the nature of its meaning mechanism, translating external messages into an internal language and vice versa (Lotman 2005, 208–209). As boundaries function as the creators, organisers and bearers of meanings they are also attributes of power (Schöpflin 2010, 65). Boundaries help identities preserve their nature and are a key aspect in giving explanations to the myth-symbol complex created and re-created by each community in their self-determination (Schöpflin 2010, 66). Thus, the boundary characterising the conflict is the main mechanism through which the unity of the *self* and the *other* can be constructed and deconstructed in descriptions. Drawing of the boundary becomes important also in constructing the characters and events represented in conspiracy narratives. Cultural semiotics differentiates between two oppositions of semiotic organisation: culture–anti-culture, and culture–non-culture. In both cases the translation function of the boundary shapes the semiotic unit (e.g. culture, text, in this case conspiracy narrative) in a way that is unique to it.

The conflict that is characterised by the opposition of culture–anti-culture is built upon the principle of mirror projection. It reflects the construction of culture and is a part of it, i.e. culture of *the own* is inconceivable without its antipode (Lepik 2007). From the point of view of the culture of the own, anti-culture is considered a highly organised structure that endangers culture. According to Lotman and Uspenskij, a tendency arises to interpret all cultures that oppose the pre-given *correct* culture as unified *incorrect* systems. Anti-culture is perceived as a culture in the negative (Lotman, Uspenskij 1978). Antithetical modelling becomes apparent vividly in a process of naming in which the names of objects reflects their nature. Thus, conspiracy theories converging around a religious conflict often directly label the conspirators as the Antichrist; in conspiracy theories connected with migration the alien component are called migrants, refugees of convenience or economic refugees (Madisson, Ventsel 2016a; Leone et al. 2020, 50), etc.

In the subchapter "The model of meaning-making on the basis of the code text of conspiracy theories", we explained how in conspiracy theories the tendency towards demonising the opposing powers becomes manifested as mirror-symmetrical binary modelling. In the case of right-wing conspiracy theories, for example, the mirror projection is manifested in the use of the discursive device of *Othered by the Other*. It represents the majority group (indigenous heterosexual males) as threatened and suppressed by minority groups (gays, feminists, childless couples, immigrants) (see Atton 2006; Madisson, Ventsel 2016b). "Often the projection precedes the mirror-projection; in other words, first, our problems are ascribed to them, and then a mirror-projective antithesis is created that opposes their problems to the 0-feature, that is, the lack of problems in our structure" (Kasekamp et al. 2019, 51, see Lepik 2007). For instance, an analysis of texts published by the Estonian populist right-wing media outlet Uued Uudised showed that these paint a black-and-white "picture of systematic and malicious subordination of traditional family values and gender roles carried out by minority groups (sexual minorities and feminists that deliberately spread misinformation) and certain left-wing intellectuals (cultural Marxists)" (Kasekamp et al. 2019, 53). Such rhetoric makes it possible to reverse typical accusations against right-wing extremists to hit their opponents and thus undermine the latter's authority and, by extension, also the criticism directed against themselves.

The anti-cultural model of self-description is first and foremost addressed at auto-communication or the self-organisation of the semiotic unit that presupposes a system closed in on itself and avoiding external influences. According to this model, the spreading of knowledge outside the system of the self can only be understood as conquering what is *incorrect* (Lotman, Uspenskij 1978, 220; Leone et al. 2020, 51). In the self-descriptions of conspiracy theorists, there is expressed an extreme desire for revelations of the activities of conspirators and to foil their nefarious plans. Signs disproving the existence of conspiracies are interpreted in a mirror-projective manner as signs of successful camouflage activities on part of the conspirators: "this is what conspirators want the public to believe". Everything that is wrong from the system's internal point of view will not become peripheral and forgotten, but will turn into anti-texts (Lotman et al. 2013, 62) – texts that in an extreme case are meant for destruction. If the conspiracy theorists do not succeed in converting signs refuting the conspiracy's existence into ones that uphold it, these are ignored or declared to be false. Drawing on Laclau and Mouffe, this opposition can be called an antagonistic situation in which antagonistic opponents do not share any common ground and a confrontation of essentialist forms of identifications or non-negotiable moral values occurs (Laclau, Mouffe 1985).

The culture–non-culture opposition, however, shapes the conflict and its parties based on a different principle that can be called an agonistic situation, proceeding from Mouffe (2005). In case of an agonistic opposition, the "we/ they" relation between conflicting parties is not so radical as it was in case of the antagonistic one. The "alien", "non-culture" are more like "adversaries", not enemies. Both sides belong to the same field of the socio-political arena, sharing a common symbolic space with certain rules within which the conflict takes place (ibid., 30). From the perspective of cultural semiotics, the outlining of the characteristic of being correct or incorrect does not point at an essential property of a semiotic unit but is connected with whether rules of forming semiotic units are followed or not. In such a type of information organisation there is no predestined and rigid structural correspondence between the languages of description and the objects described (Lotman, Uspenskij 1975) and the rules via which the world is being semiotically interpreted are themselves objects of refashioning. For instance, these rules can be the visual codes of representing the conspirators, the various discourses of describing the paralysing effects of their actions on society, etc. Thus, the conspirators' activities directed against, e.g., traditional Christian values may be seen motivated by socio-political aims, for instance the wish to promote the supremacy of LGBT values.

In case of conspiracy theories such non-discrete description of the enemy is also supported by the fact that the secrecy of the conspirators' activities plays an important role in the code text. The boundary between the own and the alien parties of the opposition is but vaguely marked here and the depiction of the characteristics of either party is largely based on non-discrete coding. It can be claimed that such a source of danger that is described in a largely non-discrete manner is mediated to a greater or lesser degree by all conspiracy theories that see the conspirators' malevolence as the force that unleashes horrible events. The conspirators' malevolence is occasionally described as so inhuman that it cannot be fully comprehended. Something inexplicable, unorganised, unstructured and unpredictable is seen in the structures of evil (Madisson 2014, 282–283), which is why it appears to be difficult to describe it precisely.

In real conspiracy narratives, both types of modelling the conflict can be present, but as the analysis below will show, one or the other can be seen to prevail in different fields.

The conspiracy narrative and the problem of the worlds of the target audience

In this book we are not observing the modelling of the conflict in conspiracy theories as just an interesting theoretical line of thought, but we are discussing it first and foremost from the perspective of strategic communication. Thus, we may ask how differentiating between these two models of conflict can be useful in a more thorough study of the strategic aims of conspiracy theories and their targeted addressees.

On the one hand, in conspiracy narratives the antithetical or agonistic modelling of conflicts points at a storyworld represented and communicated by the author of the conspiracy narrative in course of his or her discursive action. According to David Herman (2009, 106–107) storyworlds are "mental representations enabling interpreters to frame inferences about the situations, characters, and occurrences either explicitly mentioned in or implied by a narrative text or discourse. As such, storyworlds are mental models of the situations and events being recounted – of who did what to and with whom, when, where, why, and in what manner." A storyworld will begin to shape the meaning given by the interpreters to the narrative's characters and their relationships as well as events. On the other hand, the conflict represented in the narrative has to take the expectations of the targeted reader into consideration and, in principle, has to be compatible with the premises that an empirical reader might hold. Thus, the question arises about the relations between the Model Reader's world depicted in the conspiracy narrative and the real world of the targeted yet empirical reader that Eco calls the "reference world" in *Lector in Fabula*. In which ways are a world's structures translatable so that the intentions of the author of the strategic narrative might be fulfilled: the empirical readers be influenced so that they open their interpretation paths according to the strategy inserted into the Model Reader.

The world depicted in conspiracy narrative is in itself a cultural construction, but, according to Eco, so is also the empirical readers' real world or the reference world according to which they assess the verifiability of the worlds depicted in conspiracy theories. In the subchapter "The ontology of the semiotic conflict" we pointed at a cultural semiotic and discourse-theoretical perspective that in principle overlaps with the constructivist approach offered by Eco. Acknowledging of the cultural constructedness of reality here does not point at the idealist declaration of the non-existence of the "real" world. Eco treats the reader's real world as a cultural construction first and foremost in the framework of the theory of text cooperation. Comparing the activities and events occurring in the narrative "with how things are [in the real world of the empirical reader – *author's comment – M-L.M and A.V*], we are actually representing to ourselves the things that are the way they are in the form of a cultural, delimited, temporary and ad hoc construction" (Eco 2005, 140). This is valid for all the constituent parts of the reference world of the empirical reader, such as the lexicon, encyclopedia, scenarios (that were pointed out in the subchapter "Information conflicts and strategic narratives"). The reader's topical reference world thus points at any world in which characters assess and judge the worlds represented in the narrative, while both are actually socio-cultural constructions.

Postulating the reference world as culturally constructed by the reader will help us avoid judging the dangerousness of conspiracy theories and the toxicity characteristic of conspiracy theorists, or describing the so-called wholesome and rational interpretative practices that offer an alternative to conspiracy theories. Giving an unequivocally negative evaluation to conspiracy theories and connecting them with *extremism, illness, hysteria, misinformation* or *crippled epistemology*, etc., is characteristic of several discussions (see Hofstadter 1967; Pipes 1999; Sunstein, Vermeule 2009; Singer, Brooking 2018). The present analytical framework does not aim at ascertaining the psychological issues or unconscious urges of the people shaping or projecting conspiracy theories.[1] Concentrating on the perilousness of conspiracy theories will not allow for a sufficiently nuanced understanding of this phenomenon, as thus their remarkable presence in the social and cultural mainstream will, as a rule, remain unnoticed, as will their empowering potential for identity creation and play. We primarily aspire to study the potentialities of strategically formed text cooperation.

Coming back to conflict as a topic directing meaning-making, the text can presume topics or explicitly contain them, for instance, in the shape of "titles, subtitles or key phrases" (Eco 2005, 99). Still, at times the topic has to be sought after. Usually, however, a certain number of transparent *keywords* are repeated in the text that make it easier for the reader to construct the topic (Eco 2005, 98). The general character of conflict as a topic determines the way in which the properties and activities of a narrative's characters will be shaped. The strategic success of a narrative will largely depend on how aptly the narrative's creator has anticipated the reference world of the audience, the typical meaning-making tendencies prevailing in it, or, to put it more exactly, the logic of constructing the own as well as the alien elements of discourse that can follow the model of the antithesis or the agonistic conflict. The following subchapter will demonstrate how the conflict is reflected in representations of Soros-themed conspirators.

George Soros – the Grand Old Scapegoat of contemporary conspiracy narratives

"A cultural Marxist" and "a liberal", a successor of the Elders of Zion and a rootless globalist, a puppet master of the Moslem invasion and a fighter for the rights of the minorities – these are just some of the contradictory labels that George Soros has received with his actions. Soros undoubtedly is one of the favourite antiheroes of contemporary conspiracy theories. The scope of the villainous-ness attributed to him can be measured on the global scale, yet he always acquires a touch of a peculiarly local colour in particular representations. Just like the Pizzagate conspiracy theories mentioned previously, the theories targeting Soros have become notorious in recent times, for individuals influenced by these theories have conducted real attacks in order to eliminate the conspiracy. Thus, in October 2018, Cesar Sayoc sent a package containing pipe bomb to Soros by post and mailed such parcels also to other politicians and celebrities who had been criticising Donald Trump, for instance to Barack Obama and Hilary Clinton, among others.

Scholars studying conspiracy theories have even started to speak of the myth or legend of Soros. This is why the conspiracy theories concerning him are particularly well suited to serve as examples here for in each particular communication situation the shaper of a conspiracy narrative has to take into consideration the interpretative community's specific cultural context. First, we shall provide an overview of the wider background of the "Soros-themed conspiracy theories" and the formation of the Soros myth. The following subchapter presents a concise survey of the most important events appearing in the Soros-themed conspiracy theories. This is necessary to be able to proceed to analysing concrete textual strategic devices in the succeeding chapters.

George Soros and his becoming a conspiracy legend

Monitoring of disinformation (see EUvsDisInformation, Propastop;[2] Helmus et al. 2018), as well as academic studies (Colăcel, Pintilescu 2017; Kalmar et al. 2018; Krekó, Enyedi 2018; McLaughlin, Trilupaityte 2012) have noted the strategic dissemination of conspiracy theories that demonise the philanthropist of Hungarian origin. For instance, this demonisation can be done in order to vilify ideological opponents and to strengthen one's own positive image, but also just for the sake of catching or keeping the audience's attention. Naturally, avalanches of conspiracy theories painting Soros as a villain are unleashed on social media also on their own, as it were, that is without strategic interventions, but we agree with Timothy Melley that several clear-cut cases are discernible in which Soros is referred to with the aim of achieving a discrediting effect, particularly in the second half of the 2010s (Bondarenko 2017). It is remarkable that there are very different strategic actors who represent Soros as responsible for all kinds of unpleasantness, ranging from Russian disinformation sites oriented to internal as well as external audiences, the right-wing populist forces in several Central and Eastern European states to the US Republicans, to the Facebook marketing team. Academic discourse has adopted the term: the *Soros myth* (Kalmar et al. 2018) or *legend* (Colăcel, Pintilescu 2017), which indicates that the elderly billionaire is described as an antihero of superhuman power and malevolence, occasionally as a straight-out caricature of a villain whose dastardly, yet meticulously planned and systematically executed, deeds are the talk of peripheral meme sites and social media threads, as well as slogans in election campaigns. The following subchapter briefly introduces Soros's life and his becoming one of the most popular antiheroes of conspiracy theories.

The Western world knows George Soros as a US philanthropist, publicist and investor of Hungarian Jewish origin. He was born in Budapest in a German-Jewish family on 12 August 1930. His birth name was Schwartz, changed into Soros by his parents to escape anti-Semitic persecution. He managed to survive both Nazi and Communist dictatorships and emigrated to England in 1947, where he studied philosophy at the London School of Economics. Soros embarked on a successful career in finance and, in 1956, he moved to America where he specialised in European stocks. In the 1990s, Soros became famous as "the man who broke the Bank of England" as, on Black Wednesday (16 September 1992), he bet against the British pound and profited what was estimated to have been over 1 billion dollars (McLaughlin, Trilupaityte 2012,

432). Soros started his philanthropist activities in Apartheid-era South Africa in 1979, creating stipends for black South Africans to study at the University of Cape Town. In the mid-1980s he started financing foundations advancing citizen education and democracy in Central and Eastern Europe, the best-known among these is the international grantmaking network Open Society Foundations (OSF). In his birth country, Hungary, he made major investments in order to found the Central European University (CEU) and also supported many students' studies abroad. Among others, he also supported an ardent future opponent of his, as he financed the short-term studies of the Hungarian Prime Minister Viktor Orbán at the University of Oxford. In addition to investments reaching billions, Soros has been advancing a liberal democratic world view as a publicist, concentrating on the topics of minority rights, the transparency of power and the advancement of citizen society (see Krekó, Enyedi 2018).

The events in the Soros-themed conspiracy theory

Today, Soros has become the "umbrella enemy", the puppet master, allegedly pulling the strings of the *biased* mainstream media, the *corrupt* educational system, the European Union that *undermines traditional values* and *nation states* and non-profit associations, etc., that advocate *all possible kinds of minorities* (Krekó, Enyedi 2018, 48; see Colăcel, Pintilescu 2017). The Soros legend mixes the ideas of NWO, a general anti-elitism as well as anti-Semitic tropes deriving from the Protocols of the Elders of Zion and conspiracy theories connected with the Rothschilds (see Kalmar et al. 2018). Ivan Kalmar and his co-authors have identified that contemporary conspiracy theories connected with Soros contain both explicit anti-Semitism that might have been borrowed from Hitler's rhetoric, as well as implicit, deliberately hidden anti-Semitism that is understandable only to a particular segment of the audience and functions in the encoded manner of a dog whistle, as it were. An example of the latter could be the use of the echoes symbol $((()))$ in alt-right web communication. "This symbol is used in situations where a poster wishes to insinuate or point out that a person or term is either Jewish or referring to Jews" (Kalmar et al. 2018, 331). The forces that avoid Nazi analogies, e.g. mainstream right-wing populists, represent Soros as primarily the puppet master of the globalist movement whose further aim is to gain maximum power using the leverage of the deep state diluting the white, Christian nature of various nation states through immigration and Islamisation (see Vogel et al. 2018).

The Soros myth is a telling example of the contemporary networking conspiracy culture – intriguing conspiracy plots tied to a particular person have become known globally, while being promoted by popular conspiracy sites and star mediators of conspiracy theories (e.g. Alex Jones, Glenn Beck, Roseanne Barr). At the same time it is important to note that even if actors who are active in different parts of the world and bear different political aims disseminate similar or even overlapping anti-Soros conspiracy theories or the so-called global legend of Soros, the interpretations connected with this still often emerge as specific of the culture or audience in question. Neil McLaughlin and Skaidra Trilupaityte conducted a comparative study of the Soros legend in Russia, Lithuania and the US, an important conclusion of which was that internationally spreading conspiracy theories are, as a rule, interpreted proceeding from the cultural frames rooted in local politics and collective memory (2012, 432).

Below, we shall sketch briefly some of the basic events and so-called narrative anchoring points that are commonly highlighted in Soros-themed conspiracy theories. Both event and system conspiracy narratives can be found among those connected with Soros (see Barkun 2003). The former point at the billionaire as the malevolent cause of particular (easily localisable) events; the latter depict him as responsible for broader social developments, e.g. the ideas of multiculturalism infiltrating the mainstream. In the mid-1980s, or the period in which Soros started his philanthropic activities in Eastern Europe, the KGB started to disseminate conspiracy theories accusing him of espionage in favour of the US and subversive activities directed against the USSR. These theories viewed Soros and the foundations he was financing as means of brainwashing and promulgating Americanism and globalism (Kaufman 2002, 12; McLaughlin, Trilupaityte 2012, 437). Conspiracy narratives originating in Russia have also been depicting Soros as the hidden stage manager of the coloured revolutions that took place in Eastern Europe in the 2000s. A further aim of such action is supposedly the submitting of the countries that were part of the former Yugoslavia, as well as Georgia and Ukraine, to the dictate of the West (primarily the US). Russia's foreign-language (that is, addressed at a foreign audience) information and influencing channel Sputnik was one of the first sources to start connecting Soros with the apparently secret organisation of the migration crisis that shook Europe starting from the 2010s. The idea was disseminated that the crisis was called forth artificially for the sake of the Islamisation of Europe and a weakening, or downright eliminating, of the local culture (Kalmar et al. 2018, 330). The conspiracy theories addressed at Russia's internal audience represent Soros's aim as undermining of the Orthodox religion and the organisation of life proceeding from it, and the general unleashing of a chaos and immorality that would paralyse society. They even go as far as to suggest that Soros is the Antichrist or a power in the latter's service (American Antichrist and Soros ... 2019).

In conspiracy theories spreading in Catholic Eastern European countries, such as Lithuania and Poland, Soros and the organisations funded through his foundations are also depicted as undermining traditional Christian values (including gender roles, family values, etc.). There is a rather widespread motif that, under the cover of promoting citizen society and human rights, Soros is actually propagating homosexuality, abortions and drugs (see McLaughlin, Trilupaityte 2012, 440). Also, in Romania and Slovakia, Soros has been connected with the undermining of traditional gender roles; in addition, he is seen to be guilty of fanning anti-government protests and hiring people to take part in demonstrations. He has been depicted as the organiser of the anti-corruption demonstrations that started in Romania in 2015 (see Colăcel, Pintilescu 2017) and of the wave of anti-government protests in 2018 (see Mesežnikov 2019).

The dissemination of conspiracy theories strategically smearing Soros is particularly forceful in his birth country of Hungary. Similar to the conspiracy theories spreading in Russia, Soros is first and foremost depicted as an epitome of globalism and unfair capitalism as well as being responsible for its ills – poverty and inequality. The Hungarian political scientists Peter Krekó and Zsolt Enyedi have noted that conspiracy theories targeting Soros and the Central European University (CEU) founded by him, started to be spread in Hungary in 2015–2016 in the context of Europe's refugee crisis. The government led by Fidesz[3] has spent more than 100 million euros (of public funds) to convince Hungarians that Soros's aim is to bring into Europe more than a million Moslem immigrants from Asia and Africa who would imperil the local culture and way of life (Krekó, Enyedi 2018, 45). The non-profit associations financed by Soros, as well as the CEU, are seen as dangerous organisations through which he consolidates his power of influence.

Conspiracy theories similar to the above are also spreading in Estonia where they are mostly popularised by alt-right and populist forces. Such narratives underscore that the billionaire's purposeful actions have unleashed various conflicts and crises, starting from Soros promoting the coloured revolutions, up to him organising the European refugee crisis and Central American migrant caravans, as well as fomenting cultural Marxist brainwashing that will lead to a general moral decline. Quite often Soros is pointed at as one of the main instigators of the NWO conspiracy system, a top globalist who is approaching his aim of achieving maximum power via undermining nation states and the moral and intellectual degeneration of their citizens. Typically of system conspiracy theories, the dominant media outlets are seen as a propaganda mechanism of the conspirators, while social media is perceived as an unregulated information sphere that is, accordingly, more difficult to manipulate.

In America, conspiracy theories connected to Soros started spreading in the 2000s when the billionaire was openly critical of decisions made by President Bush in connection with the war in Iraq. Such theories were mostly disseminated by radical Republicans and these theories involved establishing a liberal extremist world order in which there would be no borders between nations, while hedonism and amorality of the highest degree would reign as concerns sexuality, drugs and euthanasia, as Soros's main aims (McLaughlin, Trilupaityte 2012). During Obama's presidency Soros was blamed for colluding with the President in weakening the economy of the US and establishing a socialist regime (McLaughlin, Trilupaityte 2012, 435). In connection with Donald Trump's election campaign and his period in office, the anti-Soros conspiracy theories have been intensifying and their explicitly anti-Semitic and Islamophobic versions are vigorously spreading in alt-right networks (Kalmar et al. 2018). Among other things, Soros is accused of paying for fake protests in support of feminism (e.g. the 2017 Women's March) and science, spreading false information directed against the Republicans, advocating homosuexuality and establishing a deep state that hinders transparent governance. Similar to the conspiracy theories spreading in Russia, Central and Eastern Europe, Soros's role in initiating the immigration crises is emphasised also in the USA, both in the context of the European refugee crisis as well as the Latin American immigration caravans.

In sum it could be stated that Soros's Jewish background, his enviable wealth, his philanthropic activities spinning several continents that support liberal leftist values which have been continuing for decades, as well as a relatively forceful presence in the public debates in the US and Eastern Europe, have made him one of the most important anti-heroes in contemporary conspiracy theories.

The strategic devices of the Soros-themed conspiracy narratives

This chapter aims at illustrating the model of the semiotic construction of strategic conspiracy narratives with an analysis of several conspiracy narratives connected with George Soros. We would like to give examples of topical conspiracy theories to illustrate textual strategies used by the disseminators of strategic conspiracy narratives in order to create and address their Model Reader or target audience, and show which encoding devices are being used to construct the conflict of the narrative and its constituent parties, or the opposition between *us* and *them*. We also wish to explain in the following how the code text of the conspiracy theory functions as a powerful centre that directs meaning-making and can make even seemingly separate fragments of information meaningful for an audience well versed in the base narrative and vocabulary of the Soros-themed conspiracy theory.

The study of strategic messages from the point of view of semiotics

The question of attributing intentionality is one of the most complex problems in studying strategic communication on social media. From the perspective of our model, however, this is not a question of primary importance. The strategic or goal-oriented nature of a message has been determined first and foremost by the construction of the message itself that has to take into consideration the specificity of the audience, and not the recognisability of the message's concrete constructor. With the aim of our work in mind it is not decisive whether we attribute the authorship, in the sense of being the primary source, to a creator of the message or whether this is considered the level of projection or dissemination, for our goal is to demonstrate textual devices through which the Model Author who has been created discursively, "justifies the actions and shapes the meanings of conflicts in public sphere and influence the audience behaviour in a way desired" (O'Loughlin et al. 2017, 50). If the researcher manages to detect unity in the aims of different narratives, both the levels of formation as well as of projection will fulfil the same function in influencing the audience. The levels merge together in the Model Author who can adopt various guises, e.g. the Government's press representative, an expert, an influencer on social media, but whose unity can still be constructed via the aims and the agenda being disseminated through the narratives. Is it really important here which source was the first to mention the conspiracy theories? What is more, often strategic actors (e.g. the Hungarian government led by Orbán) will pick up a conspiracy theory already in circulation and make it into a constituent part of their own strategic communication. Who is the first strategic author in such a case?

One of the preconditions for constructing the Model Author is that in the asymmetric strategic communication on social media, a strategic actor cannot start constructing and disseminating narratives that are in conflict with his or her real aims, e.g. Orbán cannot advance a public narrative in which he would accuse the European Union of spreading Soros-themed conspiracy theories. As it is difficult for the creator to control the further spread of narratives on social media, the contradictions in the narratives referred to could bring along undesired communicative results for Orbán as a strategic actor, as he would partly be legitimising Soros's agenda.

Neither are we analysing the reception level nor taking a stance on the success of the textual strategies used in conspiracy narratives as concerns manipulation. For this purpose, qualitative audience research should be conducted, which remains outside the focus of this book. However, in analysing our examples we can indicate which strategic aims and communicative functions a device *could* bear for an audience that shares certain cultural codes and pragmatic standards. What is more, this admission is connected with a constitutive characteristic of the humanities. As stated by Boris Uspenskij, a leading figure of the Tartu-Moscow School of Semiotics, "Nothing whatsoever can be proven in humanities that study human culture. We can only explain one phenomenon or another, while one and the same phenomenon can be explained in manners that are in principle different. The degree of convincingness of one or another explanation is determined by relating of the phenomena, that is, the measure to which one or another explanation would allow us to interpret other phenomena contingent with the one observed" (Uspenskij 2013, 23). The main contribution of our semiotic treatment thus is the revealing of particular textual strategies employed in constructing the Model Reader and explicating their success potential. The examples given in the analysis have been chosen with this aim in mind and do not cover the full plethora of devices characteristic of Soros-themed conspiracy narratives.

We are focusing on three separate thematic fields of the strategic narrative that nevertheless are remarkably interwoven. First, there are political narratives whose main purpose is to form a political agenda, to undermine the opponent's positions or image, and to construct a political community. As was pointed out in the subchapter "The functions of identity creation in conspiracy theories", by "political", we first and foremost mean the logics of the signification processes in social relationships through which attempts are made to solve or shape social oppositions and conflicts. Here, conspiracy narratives mostly fulfil the symbolic function of identity creation.

Second, there are conspiracy theories that embody alternative knowledge that question the discourse via institutionalised discourses that are (re)produced by these institutions (e.g. the dominant system of education). Such dominant discourses attempt to make the way in which things are discussed natural and thus the power relationship of these discourses is based on silent authority. Conspiracy theorists often see their mission as undermining the norms of political correctness propagated by mainstream media, the education system and the state institutions (Madisson 2016b), while they are also trying to offer alternative knowledge discourses in return. Proceeding from Foucault, the latter can be conceptualised as subjugated knowledge. The French thinker takes subjugated knowledge to appear in historical contents that have been disqualified in power games as formally unsystematised, non-conceptual, insufficiently elaborated, naïve, located low down in hierarchy, beneath the required level of specialist knowledge or scientificity (Foucault 1980, 82). At the same time, this subjugated knowledge is *not* general, common-sense knowledge; on the contrary, it is particular, local, differential knowledge which is never unanimous and which owes its force only to the harshness with which it is opposed by everything surrounding it (Foucault 1980, 82). As the determination of the dominant discourse greatly depends on the context with which it is being compared, in the present case it is the perspective of the conspiracy theorists' positive self-description that is important. Often, conspiracy theorists see themselves as true enlightenment figures, as they usually understand mainstream media as a sphere of conspiratorial propaganda, disinformation and/or mind control "and that their conspiracist beliefs are literally revolutionary in their political and epistemological implications" (Ballinger 2011, 73; see also Hristov 2019).

Third, we zoom in on conspiracy narratives used for marketing purposes that serve the function of a general catching of attention and infotainment, as well as the advancement of concrete personal brands. In addition, we analyse the application of conspiracy theories in PR, concentrating on an example in which an attempt was made to use strategic dissemination of conspiracy theories to delegitimise criticism directed against a large corporation.

Conspiracy theories connected with Soros embrace all these fields and often a conspiracy narrative and its internal textual devices can bear a number of different functions. For instance, conspiracy theorists see achieving political supremacy as the main aim of Soros's actions, while his foundations are pointed at as a mechanism to that end via which the billionaire "naturalises" liberal democratic views in the system of education. Thus, the boundaries between the thematic fields of conspiracy narratives are relative and which function will become predominant is dependent on the particular communication situation and the adopted aim. The examples chosen have been collected from different sources: we use reports compiled by portals fighting disinformation and academic studies which include articles by other scholars, as well as our own earlier qualitative studies.

Political conspiracy narrative: formation of the figure of external enemy

This subchapter focuses first on examples of political conspiracy theories connected with Soros in which the aim of constructing a common external enemy is the legitimisation of one's own foreign political agenda and transformation of a home conflict into a foreign political topic. Here, we observe how pro-Russia narratives create connections of alliance in the context of events occurring in Ukraine, Georgia and Armenia. After that we analyse conspiracy narratives connected with Soros that primarily aim at undermining the political elite or delegitimising the political opposition and whose other, more concrete aim is the shaping and mobilising of a targeted audience. Naturally, the examples given can fulfil all the functions but for the sake of clarity we have differentiated them in our analysis.

We start our analysis with four conspiracy narratives that are aimed at different target audiences. Mostly, our examples derive from the website of the portal EUvsDisInformation[4] that is dedicated to exposing disinformation directed against the European Union emanating from Russia. It gives examples of dozens of conspiracy theories disseminated by RT, Sputnik and other Russian media channels that construct the malevolent activities of the US and Soros as the main conflict, yet each subconflict takes into consideration the concrete political situation and cultural background. We start by quoting the Russian political scientist Araik Stepanjan, who belongs to the Russian Academy's scientific council dealing with geopolitical problems and frequently appears on the Russian television channels Rossija 1 and Rossija 2.[5]

> The goal of the US is to create chaos, so that the Orthodox would kill one another – Ukrainians would kill Ukrainians, Georgians would kill Georgians, they are also working in Armenia. It is the Antichrist that came into our home. It is the network of Soros, which does not care about nations, religions, God or the devil – they are sowing chaos in post-Soviet space.

This may be the most comprehensive example of Soros's heinous actions, but a similar conspiracy narrative can be found on different media channels financed by the Russian state. An article published by the RT on 5 July 2019, "The government bears full responsibility: The Soros Foundation urging Tbilisi authorities to fight against the Russian Federation's 'hybrid war' against Georgia" points at the activities of the Soros foundation as the main escalator of protests against Russia.[6] Among the foundation's activities in 2019, the article mentions other projects, costing hundreds of thousands of dollars, whose goal is to counter "Russian disinformation" and the negative reconceptualisation of the Soviet past (Gureeva, Lužnikova 2019). This conspiracy theory contains intertextual references to other, similar conspiracy theories that hold George Soros responsible for secretly organising and sponsoring anti-government protest actions in several post-Soviet states. The use of inverted commas ("") attributes the status of ridiculous statements to "Russian disinformation" and Russia's "hybrid war" against Georgia. The use of inverted commas is a device that was employed already by Soviet press when it was necessary to direct the readers' attention to the legitimacy of the opponent's claims (see Papernyi 1996).

We provide a couple of additional examples about the Soros-themed conspiracy theories spreading in the post-Soviet space, an aim of which is to construct an external enemy. The RT programme "CrossTalk Bullhorns: Crazy world" with Dmitry Babich, John Laughland, and Alex Christoforou on 13 May 2019 spoke, regarding the connections between Ukraine's new president Volodymyr Zelensky and Soros, that the President and numerous members of his team are stooges of George Soros and the Liberals (CrossTalk … 2019). The Italian-language Sputnik, that disseminates a similar, in principle pro-Kremlin, agenda continued the narrative and claimed at the beginning of July 2019 that George Soros destabilises states in order to provoke civil wars like Euromaidan in the Ukraine (Statello 2018). In the case of both examples linked with the Ukraine, Soros is represented as the main puppet master whose influence on the new president could escalate the political climate within Ukraine into a war.

An article from Sputnik Armenia (Dispute between … 2019) tells us that the Soros Foundation is plotting the destruction of Armenia. In addition, the Soros Foundation is organising confrontations in Armenia as Soros's accomplices encourage the Armenians to come out against the people of Artsakh (Nagorno-Karabakh): "They want civil war and blood."

Dominant textual strategies

In the following we will observe the main textual devices that have been used in these examples to construct the Model Reader. In these cases, the conflict has been built with inferences from one type of ordinary scenarios – war scenarios. This determines the choice and meaning of the basic vocabulary and a certain framework of action for the participants in the narrative. The events that took place in Ukraine, Georgia and Armenia in 2018–2019 are framed in a war scenario and a Model Reader is created who activates and directs the empirical reader towards attributing meaning to today's conflicts in the light of previous ones. Earlier experiences of civil war in these countries ("Ukrainians would kill Ukrainians, Georgians would kill Georgians", "provoke civil wars like Euromaidan in Ukraine")[7] as well as conflicts with neighbouring countries ("They want the Armenians to come out against the people of Artsakh (Nagorno-Karabakh)")[8] are recalled. A war scenario also determines the activities of the characters belonging to Soros's network: intelligence networks are hinted at who operate under cover and serve the interests of foreign states. Secret subversion agents are implied that seek to undermine traditional values.

The disseminators of messages perceived as fake information are presented as information warriors who spread anti-Russia attitudes and distort the picture of a mutual past when Georgia used to belong to the Soviet Union. Then, the Model Reader is guided to creating connections with the narratives of rewriting history.

Such conspiracy theories underline the ongoing desire on part of Western media to minimise Russia's cultural but, first of all, political role in history. This sequence of conspiracy theories also includes theories about historians bribed by the West who will not recognise the leading role of the Soviet Union in defeating Hitler's Germany; as well as those concerning scholars who suggest that the Baltic States did not voluntarily join the Soviet Union but were occupied in 1940, etc. In connection with the popular TV series Chernobyl (2019), conspiracy theories have emerged as to the *real* reasons for the catastrophe involving the infiltration of CIA agents in the personnel of the nuclear power plant and subversive action on their part. The basic plot of rewriting history mentioned above could be considered one of the most widespread theories of an anti-Russian conspiracy on Russian media (Rebane 2018).

One of the strategic aims of the use of the war scenario is the creation of a situation of military tension under conditions in which there is no actual war. According to Lev Gudkov, Russian sociologist and director of the analytical Levada Centre, in case of war the main aims of discursive activities of adversaries consist of the demonisation of a concrete enemy and mobilisation of people to fight (Gudkov 2005, 14). Such a war framework tends to be built upon a narrative strategy based on continual modelling in Lotman's sense, in which the causal relationships between particular events are not disclosed, but only indicated as analogies. Rather, the creating of relationships occurs on the basis of external similarities. On the level of discourse, one of the possibilities of activating such continuous creation of relationships is the code text of conspiracy discourse that represents the large-scale conspiratorial actions of "the figure of the enemy" – in this particular case, Soros. "The figure of the enemy" is characterised by ideological and dogmatic construction and irrationality. It is a product of propaganda used to demonise a political and ideological enemy, with the purpose of legitimating its advocate's own pretensions of power (Buchbender 1989, 18). The author of a strategic narrative has to use stereotypes and images of threat that can characterise the figure of an enemy of the target audience. What is involved in this particular case includes hints at a war scenario, concrete experiences of war the audience may have experienced in the course of history, etc. The Soros-themed conspiracy narrative provides unified explanations to subconflicts or subtopics that otherwise appear as separate and guides the Model Reader towards making connections between the subconflicts, which makes Soros everyone's omnipotent mutual enemy.

The war scenario is based on antithetical meaning-making that clearly divides the conflict into two opposing parties divided by an uncrossable boundary and is supported by other strategies of rhetorical and stylistic hyper-coding connected with war. Thus, parallels are drawn between Soros's activities and occupation, the results of his villainous deeds are represented as bloody and destabilising, in line with war, etc. Inferences from intertextual scenarios activate cultural texts in the target audience that present Soros's actions in the framework of a biblical contestation between Good and Evil, in which Soros appears as "Antichrist that came into our home" (see above for Araik Stepanjan's speech). Intertextual scenarios overlap with ideological targeting that, according to Eco, will take into consideration the probable ideological views of the empirical reader (Eco 2005, 92). In these examples the ideological references of the Model Reader are connected to a conservative, (Orthodox) world view that cherishes traditional family values which are represented as endangered. According to the scholar of conspiracy theories Mark Fenster, contemporary popular eschatology is characterised by a tendency to divide reality into an antithesis of good and evil, which is superimposed upon an historical narrative that attempts to make sense of the natural via the supernatural. The world is experienced as a setting for secret and dangerous events where danger to Christian beliefs and values being undermined keeps lurking continually (Fenster 2008, 228).

Functions

Dissemination of the conspiracy narrative that is constructed on the basis of the ordinary war scenario, religious intertextual scenarios, and ideological hypercodings bears several interconnected functions. First, it helps to shape the targeted audience and the horizon of interpretation prevailing there, which is characterised by an interpretation frame that models the world in a black and white manner. Creating an interpretative community contains references to certain historical events (in this case, hints at war events) that start to guide the reader's further interpretations and the logic of creating a possible chain of events in the capacity of subtopics. The code-textual logic of conspiracy theories helps the strategic actor create a Model Reader who has a unified enemy in Soros. Recognising Soros as the cause of different events and subconflicts makes it possible to treat the readers who identify with these events as a potentially unified targeted audience, or one of the political-strategic characteristics of such a narrative is the expansion of the target audience.

Second, from the perspective of strategic communication it is equally important to mark the position of *us* that makes it possible for the author of the narrative, in addition to targeting the audience, to achieve goals related to the political agenda. The actions and aims of the Model Author, i.e. the discursive position of *us*, need not always be explicit in strategic narrative as this may diminish the credibility of the forwarded information and create a feeling of being manipulated in the audience. Thus, the justified question arises as to how it is possible to construct a unified Model Author, a strategic actor, proceeding from all these examples? Taking into consideration that the Model Author appears as a result of the text's interpretative cooperation, we as researchers will be able to detect signs pointing at the strategic goals of the narratives on the level of discourse. In discourses this is indicated, on the one hand, by the actions taken by *us* in the solving of the conflict. The Sputnik Armenia article saw banning of the foundations as a key to conflict solving: "The foundation workers and people cooperating with them are foreign agents. Therefore, the foundation's office in Armenia must be closed. Their activities should be prohibited" (Dispute between … 2019). Such counteractions suggested as solutions to subconflicts can help the researcher to construct the Model Author and his or her political aims to which the audience's support is sought with the help of narratives. We can see that, in addition to constructing the external enemy, one of the narrative's aims is directed at the delegitimisation of internal political opponents: the unrest may be initiated externally, but its actualisation is being helped by Soros's minions.

Another possibility is to derive the goals, using antithetical mirror-projective logic: Soros's villainous plans go counter to the position of *us* or the Model Author. In a situation where the strategic actor cannot openly reveal his or her goals such an indirect reading can offer a key to detecting the text's real goals and the position of the possible real actor (see also Ventsel et al. 2019). Although in constructing the Model Reader the specific socio-cultural background of the target audience is taken into account, a surprising unity emerges in the narrative's main agenda in case of our examples: all of these connect Soros with organising pro-Western demonstrations and question the legitimacy of such meetings. At times there are direct indications of this: "the Soros Foundation serves foreign interests in Armenia" points at Soros as the arch-enemy. As the mutual enemy is taking shape, so is its opposite part – the common *us*. According to the logic of antithetical reading, an enemy of Soros's should be our friend. Thus, Russia, against whom Soros is also waging war in Georgia ("Soros foundation called for Tbilisi's [i.e. Georgian authorities – *authors' comment* A.V, M-L.M] opposition to Russia's 'hybrid war' against Georgia" (Gureeva, Lužnikova 2019)), can clearly be positioned as belonging to the *us* represented in the Model Author. There are also other signs that allow us to see Russia's foreign political agenda behind these examples. In the Armenian case, referring to Nagorno-Karabakh functions as an indirect hint at Russian foreign politics whose support has helped Armenia to maintain an autonomous enclave with an Armenian population within Azerbaijan.

With such a frame of analysis we are able to detect a certain unity in different aims that are being sought via these narratives. A common aim makes it possible to construct a Model Author behind these texts for, as we identified in the subchapter "Information conflicts and strategic narratives", the Model Author is formed in strategic communication through the unity of the aims set by the narratives. These must not be in conflict with one another. In this case the indirect signs used in reflecting the events in Ukraine, Georgia and Armenia point at Russia as a strategic actor.

Political conspiracy narrative: opposition to the elite

In exemplifying the textual strategies of anti-elitist conspiracy narratives related with Soros, we mostly rely on analysing conspiracy theories circulating in right-wing populist Estonian media. The Soros-themed conspiracy theories circulating in former post-Soviet countries are remarkably different from one another. Thus, McLaughlin and Trilupaityte (2012, 439) indicate in an article mapping the Soros-themed conspiracy theories, that in Lithuania the heated attacks on Soros and his foundation were ultimately not about the Jewish billionaire, but mainly stood out as attempts to undermine local political and intellectual figures by linking them to the notorious donor. The conspiracy theories suggest that under cover of supporting the civil society Soros helped the old establishment settle in high positions in the new conditions of the re-independent Lithuania (Radžvilas 2008). So, the main conflict here has been encoded as an ideological battle between ex-communists and non-communists, while it is interesting that Soros's name is linked to the aspirations of those formerly in power. Differently from Lithuania, in the Estonian context it is not former communists who have been marked as Soros's supporters, and there are virtually no suggestions of a religious ideological hypercoding that in the Baltic context can be found in Lithuania (McLaughlin, Trilupaityte 2012). Still, both Estonian as well as Lithuanian conspiracy theories almost never point at Soros as an organiser of real uprisings and nodes of military conflict that could be pointed at in the Ukrainian, Georgian and Armenian contexts.

The malevolent actions belonging to the fabula of the main Soros-themed conspiracy theories spreading in Estonia depict Soros and his minions as bent on destroying the political organisation of life that is based on the notion of the nation state (Rahvusriikide lammutaja ... 2019). Soros's manipulations are first and foremost connected with the influence of the politics of the European Union and fanning various subconflicts. The figure of Soros as the anti-hero reached Estonia more noticeably in 2015 when a discourse arose depicting him as the source of the migration crisis that had hit Europe and, according to the conspiracy theorists, had been called forth deliberately with the aim of destroying nation states. Uued Uudised, the main organ of the extreme right-wing Conservative People's Party of Estonia (EKRE)[9] constructs the conflict initiated by Soros in the following way (Kui Trump Soros ... 2018):

> Some days ago, the Voice of Europe wrote about the Soros Express or the migration crisis financed by the scandalous billionaire and destroyer of nation states George Soros which is wholly artificial. Namely, both the Balkan and the Mediterranean migration routes have been set in motion deliberately, while a Central American route has been added to these as well that is intended for putting pressure on Donald Trump's administration.

In the conspiracy narratives concerning Estonia, Soros's minions mostly include the local political establishment that has been suggested to include active participants in institutionalised politics, opinion leaders who mostly represent liberal democratic views, as well as the educational system. Soros's purported manipulations have been nicely summarised in the blog Rahvuslane that is popular with the Estonian alt-right and, on 12 May 2018, shared a piece by Tiit

Madisson, a dissident and conspiracy theorist well known in Estonia, titled "Jewish 'revolutionaries' refashioning the world",

> In 1998 the political cream of Estonia, whose fawning upon the powerful of this world was nigh unfathomable, in the person of President (Lennart Meri) awarded George Soros with the Order of the Cross of Terra Mariana, apparently for furthering democracy. In case of Soros, however, this is expressed as violent merging of nations, destroying of classic human morals and national cultures, eradicating humanity and a natural atmosphere for life and natural human relationships, and other activities detrimental to the nation state.
>
> (Tiit Madisson 2018)

Dominating textual strategies

The main conflict incited by Soros is constructed by the Estonian extreme right audience primarily in the framework of political and nationalist *ideological hypercoding*. This greatly determines the nature of the basic lexicon (actions, actors) building the discourse and other ways of encoding. The narrative of Soros as the destroyer and annihilator of nation states is connected with actions instigated by him and his minions that aid the mixing of nationalities and the accompanying downfall of nation states (the migration crisis in Europe and America).

The phrase "the Soros Express" is used to describe the migration streams purportedly caused by Soros, and functions as a specific rhetorical-stylistic code in the target audience (Ungari hoiatab ... 2018). "The Soros Express" refers to the migration streams that have been deliberately set in motion and that Soros is using to catch media attention, provoke national governments and stir conflicts. It is also emphasised that in public the dastardly Jewish billionaire presents his manipulations achieved with the help of migrants as activities spurred on by humanist considerations. In the opinion of conspiracy theorists, the real aim of such influencing activities is to escalate the conflict to a degree in which states would abandon their right to defend their borders against migrants who wish to enter the country. From the perspective of text creation strategies, the migration crisis called into life by Soros functions as a discursive subtopic, a subconflict. It guides the target audience towards treating Soros's actions as part of the bigger plan to destroy nation states as such.

The above-quoted excerpts, particularly that by Tiit Madisson, demonstrate that the figure of the enemy has been constructed on the basis of an antithetically modelled conflict: Soros's actions are described in a binary mirror projection as activities endangering "the natural", i.e. the only order possible. "Classic morals", "a natural atmosphere for living" and "nation state" are encoded rhetorically as concepts on the same level, which results in attributing the characteristic of "naturalness" to the concept of "nation state". Thus, Soros's supposed battle against nation states is also a battle against the humans' natural socio-political way of life. Intertextual encoding connects Soros with Jewish revolutionaries, which in the Estonian cultural sphere primarily points at connotations with the Bolshevik world revolution that bears a clearly negative meaning in the public space.

Functions

In the case of these examples it is important on the strategic level that readers should become used to the explanatory model that sees the local (political) elite of Estonia, which purportedly supports Soros's agenda and has been bribed by him, as a destructive force that represents a danger to Estonians as well as to Estonia as a nation state. This became obvious before the parliamentary elections of 2019: "Soros's troll factory aka the Open Estonia Foundation has started meddling in the elections for the Riigikogu, attempts to dictate election topics and to influence the election results by libelling those forces that defend national and traditional values" (Rahvusriikide lammutaja … 2019).

In addition to sketching the figure of the enemy, the analysed examples also contain clear-cut hints at a world that helps the researchers detect the possible strategic aims present in the examples. It appeared above that, on the one hand, the position of *us* is characterised by an agenda of the nation state corresponding to "the natural order of things" that Soros's malignant actions attempt to destroy. Via an antithetical reading the researcher can in principle derive the characteristics of both parties. We have been describing this when also studying other Estonian alt-right conspiracy theories that present their values through binary oppositions as *moral, natural, rational and traditional*, while the opponents are described as *amoral, unnatural, irrational and loose* forces led by *unbridled hedonism, selfishness and a desire to do evil* (see Madisson, Ventsel 2016a, 333; Madisson 2016a).

From time to time concrete steps are proposed that should be taken against Soros's actions, i.e. serve as means to solve the conflict: "The first step would be to make clear to the European public how, why and what exactly the open society funds and Soros are doing so that the attempts to turn his destructive fantasy into a political consensus or normality for the masses could be hindered in course of an informed debate" (George Soros … 2016). Concrete proposals, and countermeasures against Soros's actions that are being referred to in the narratives, also function as references to the boundaries of the position and identity of *us*.

On the other hand, the position of the Model Author can be detected from the "fellow sufferers" – our allies are the US led by Donald Trump and, within Europe, first and foremost Orbán's Hungary whose political value world is similar to *ours*. We learn from the alternative media channel Objektiiv, which is popular with the Estonian national conservative and even extreme right circles, that Soros "keeps visiting Brussels to bargain for a punishment for Orbán" (Soros saalib Brüsseli vahet … 2018) and from the

Tiit Madisson article "This activity [sanction against Hungary – *authors' comment* M-L.M, A.V] is unfortunately supported also by Estonia's power elite, a loyal poodle of the leaders of the European Union" (Tiit Madisson 2018). We can see that two opposing sides are taking shape: on the one side there is Soros, the European Union, the local Estonian elite; and on the other side there are local right-wing populist political forces and (ultra)nationally-minded target audiences as well as Hungary, Orbán and Trump who are being added together as victims of Soros's malicious actions by the conspiracy theory's code text.

Political conspiracy narrative: opposing ideological adversaries

Finally, we analyse political conspiracy narratives related to Soros with the help of which the political forces in power attempt to legitimise their power ambitions and undermine the political agenda of their opponents. The example of Hungary was already introduced at the beginning of the previous subchapter. Presumably, Hungary is the country in which Soros's image has been at the centre of political life for the longest period of time, in the most varied ways and also in the most intensive manner (Krekó, Enyedi 2018, 46). At times he has been used in strategic communication very successfully. According to a poll conducted in Hungary in 2018, 51 per cent of respondents believed that the migration crisis of 2015 had been initiated by Soros and his stooges (Hungary: Europe's champion ... 2018). Also, those opposing Orbán believed that Soros wanted to conquer Europe with the help of Moslems (ibid.).

In the following we shall mostly concentrate on the example of Hungary as, since 2015, in that country "the government has spent more than 100 million euros to convince voters that a hidden network led by George Soros" exists (Krekó, Enyedi 2018, 45). A textbook example of how party-political interests are being channeled into a cultural opposition between the own and the alien is the "Stop Soros" package initiated by the Orbán government that attempts to pass its agenda as a manifestation of the will of the people. On 13 February 2018, Zsolt Semjén, the Deputy Prime Minister of Hungary, filed a package of bills on behalf of the government which consisted of three different bills: (1) Bill T/19776 on the permits for organisations supporting migration; (2) Bill T/19774 on the immigration restraint order; and (3) Bill T/19775 on the immigration funding fee (Boros 2018). All three were concerned with fighting migration and their goal was to restrict the activities of various NGOs whose stance on migration politics differed from that of the government. In the words of the Hungarian political analyst Tamás Boros "The government claims that all attempts at helping migration constitute a national security risk and must be countered accordingly. It considers all migration policies or activities that contravene its own policy as dangerous, and regards George Soros as the main financier of these threats" (2018).

Dominant textual strategies

The goal of the anti-Soros campaign has been to promote what the Prime Minister of Hungary Victor Orbán and the leader of Poland's ruling Law and Justice party Jarosaw Kaczyñski called a "cultural counter-revolution" in 2016 (Krekó, Enyedi 2018, 45). The name contains two text-strategic moves: on the one hand, an attempt is made to present the anti-Soros campaign in the framework of a cultural conflict; on the other hand, the activities are being legitimised as revolutionary. In the former case the Model Reader is being guided to read the politics of the Orbán government not as a campaign for the narrow private interests of a single party, but as a fight for the preservation of the cultural identity of each and every Hungarian. Historically, *revolution* has stood for a fight against the regime in power. In this case, however, the fight against a political regime is being transformed into a cultural revolution, in which the Fidesz Party led by Orbán is entering a crusade against the cultural establishment that has been allegedly infiltrating different Hungarian institutions and poisoning Hungarian "hearts and minds" during previous decades. Pointing at a revolution amplifies the scope of Orbán's political agenda even more: the revolution is not happening because of a party's private interests but is being represented as something embracing the whole society and thus manifesting the will of the people. Revolutionary events are mostly depicted as an activity on the grassroots level of ordinary citizens and not as actions initiated from above, which is why Orbán is represented as an authentic representative of the Hungarian people.

With this textual strategy the Model Reader is guided onto an interpretative path that represents the opponents of the cultural revolution as forces also opposed to the will of the people. Thus, Figyelő, a Christian-conservative Hungarian business magazine, published a list of more than 200 people (mainly academics and human-rights activists) whom it called "mercenaries" hired by Soros (Krekó, Enyedi 2018, 46). Soros's minions are depicted as bribable, i.e. the self-image of the Model Author is getting an opponent in the image of an enemy whose actions are motivated by monetary calculations. A similar opinion can be read on Orbán's official website that describes Soros as " 'an American financial speculator' whose 'power, size, and weight' was greater than that of all of Hungary, and who was 'ruining the lives of millions of European people with his financial speculations' " (Kalmar et al. 2018, 4). Even more obviously, Orbán creates a connection between the avarice of Soros's supporters and an ordinary criminal scenario in one of his radio interviews: "These activists who support immigrants inadvertently become part of this international human-smuggling network" (Gergely 2015). Adding a code of criminality to the Model Reader is a strategic move in order to expand the limits the of the interpretative community. It directs the doubtful part of the audience for whom Orbán's anti-Soros actions lack legitimacy as a fight for culture towards interpreting Soros's activities in the light of a code of criminality and illegality.

Constructing such a cultural conflict that embraces the whole of society allows Orbán to use intertextual encodings based on different historical analogies when he is constructing his own Model Reader. In a speech given during this election campaign 2018, one of the aims of which was to collect support to the "stop Soros package", Orbán created connections between Soros's manipulations and key events in Hungarian history: "We sent home the [Ottoman] sultan with his army, the Habsburg kaiser with his raiders and the Soviets with their comrades", "Now we will send home Uncle George" (Conspiracy theories about ... 2018). Orbán's rhetoric shapes a Model Reader who is familiar with important intertextual references to Hungarian history (the invasion of the Ottoman Empire, the Habsburgs, the Soviets) and is able to identify with those. In addition, vocabulary is used that is familiar to the older generation: "Uncle George" refers to America, primarily as a globalist economic superpower that sabotages a world order based on sovereignty and undermines cultural plurality. The historical analogies that are largely based on war scenarios and boost national pride depict today's fight against Soros as an epic war for the national and cultural survival and sovereignty of Hungarians.

The conflict constituting the "counter-cultural revolution" is constructed most directly as a "clash of civilisations" between the patriotic defenders of a traditional Christian nation and "international forces" that want to repopulate Europe with Africans. Andras Aradszki, a Hungarian politician and member of the National Assembly for Érd and a Member of the Parliament delivered an address in the Parliament of Hungary on 9 October 2017 titled, "The Christian duty to fight against the Satan/Soros Plan" (Novak 2017). From the perspective of constructing the Model Author it is important that a connection be made between Hungarian identity and a Christian intertextual code that makes it possible to place the struggle into a world historical perspective and see in the events of the moment manifestations of a conflict that transcends civilisations. At the same time, it is indicated that the enemy is first and foremost an intruder, an external danger who is to be countered by internal forces: "We will fight against the Soros empire" (ibid.; see also Conspiracy theories about ... 2018). The mobilising call to fight against the Soros empire sets the latter side by side with such powerful intruders as the Ottoman, Habsburg and Soviet empires. Yet similarly to the historical empires, also Soros has its agents who are pulling the threads within Hungary and implementing anti-Hungarian policies (NGOs, the CEU).

As an additional strategy of the ideological encoding of the Model Reader, the covert use of an anti-Semitic discourse can be pointed at in Orbán's rhetoric. For instance, the "stop Soros" package campaign was accompanied by billboards all over the country saying, "We shall not let Soros have the last laugh." Deborah Lipstadt, Professor of Holocaust history at Emory University has said that "No one [explicitly] says Soros is a Jew, but there are groups on the right for whom these [symbols] are a wink-wink, nod-nod dog whistle" (Weaver, Hopkins 2018; see also Kalmar et al. 2018). Such encoding is particularly significant for an audience who is aware of the trope of the "Laughing Jew" appearing in the Hitler-era Nazi rhetoric. In this way, "Orbán was able to position himself close enough to the voters of the extreme right, but not so close as to lose the mainstream respectability that, even in Hungary, excludes open and deliberate antisemitism" (Kalmar et al. 2018, 5).[10]

Functions

The main strategic aims of the narratives shaped by Orbán's supporters include shaping a conflict that would channel party-political differences of opinion into an opposition of cultural identity between Hungarians and their opponents who are manipulated by Soros. On the one hand, it can be said that the fight against Soros as a person does not serve as the main aim of the strategic narratives because Soros does not participate directly in a Hungarian internal political election campaign. However, connections with Soros and his supposed plans that endanger the cultural and historical heritage of Hungary make it possible to delegitimise the forces that oppose Orbán's political agenda and justify his own particular activities that serve as attempts to solve the conflict (e.g. prohibiting of NGOs, passing an anti-migration act, etc.). On the other hand, first and foremost considering the textual strategic aims, the discourse shapes a Model Author (supporters of Orbán and his agenda) that unites in itself events important from the perspective of the national narrative. This makes it possible to expand the potential interpretative community as the Model Reader is led towards identifying not so much with Orbán and his Fidesz Party but rather with events and actors important from the perspective of communal cultural memory.

On the level of discourse the code-textual logic of such conspiracy narrative allows viewing different discrete activities as justified constituent parts of a larger whole. The "Stop Soros" package, that was first and foremost directed at silencing the forces opposing Orbán's politics, was rhetorically constructed as a revolutionary and nationalistic protest of Hungarians against Soros's criminal machinations that bring about cultural destruction. The narrative of an endangered nation that has found a central place in Orbán's rhetoric will make it possible to legitimise means taken to hinder the opponents' actions even in the future, as the code-textual logic of the Soros-themed conspiracy theory allows classification under its label of different actions that can be shown as endangering the Hungarian cultural identity.

As was already said at the beginning of this analysis, conspiracy narratives can bear different functions and the issue here is rather the domination of a function. This is so also in the case in which the main target audience of Orbán's rhetoric is domestic. Yet the larger the segment of the potential target audience that can be discursively addressed with the help of the Model Reader, the more wide-reaching should be the represented conflict with which the audience should be able to identify. Thus, the fight for Christian values makes it possible to create connections with other political forces using similar rhetoric in both internal as well as foreign politics. For many anti-EU forces, Orbán's Hungary serves as a model due to its anti-Brussels rhetoric. This is why the forming of such a camp clearly is one of the aims of the strategic author, as it makes it possible to get positive feedback to its actions from international actors who emphasise similar values.

Conspiracy narrative of alternative knowledge: representing a decadent conspiracy system

How is the dominant Western world view to be delegitimised? How to undermine the understanding of the "natural order" of things and basic humanist values? These are questions that we shall attempt to answer by showing the role of the Soros-themed conspiracy narratives in constructing conflicts of world views. Also, the previous chapter that directly focused on the narratives of events and identities that undermine the image of political opponents talked about the war of civilisations and the purported unnaturalness of the value systems cultivated by Soros. This part primarily concentrates on discourses in which the specific conflict of world views, the events constituting the narrative and the parties involved do not stand out in so strong relief. This is understandable for the theme of these strategic narratives is a dominating system of media and education, that supposedly promotes liberal leftist ideology, as a whole. The conspiracy theories concentrating on knowledge represent their own value system as knowledge that is being subjected to the system of the mainstream, while the reason for such marginalisation and relegation to the periphery is seen in Soros's actions. Another difference in political conspiracy narratives in many ways derives from the previous point – their targeted audience is relatively diffuse. Constructing a conflict as the main mechanism for creating a strategic interpretative community is represented in a more latent manner, which is why the boundaries between *the own* and *the alien* appear as less clearly drawn discursively. Based on examples from Estonian and Hungarian right-wing populist media discourse, we demonstrate the logic of the narrative of a global conspiracy system and of the latent conflict characteristic of the latter.

Narratives that are centred around the idea of malignant propagation of dangerous and unnatural ideologies in the education system and the media can undoubtedly be described as the type of system narratives that were discussed in subchapter "The semiotic approach to conspiracy narratives". Their timeline reaches back beyond decades and they embrace complex series of events as well as multiple actors, ranging from individuals seen as embodiments of evil (Soros, Hillary Clinton, Pope Francis) and local institutions (particular individuals, media outlets, banks) up to large international organisations (the EU, the UN, Amnesty International). It is important to emphasise that such narratives speaking of a decadent global conspiracy system represent an influential structure of evil that is successfully permeating the social fabric and is hierarchical; it is presumed that many socially influential persons and structures serve the aims of the conspirators. At the same time, it is also presumed that the bottom layers of the conspiracy pyramid participate in the pernicious system without being aware of this. Such explanations see knowledge that obscures people's critical thinking and blurs the so-called natural values as an indispensable lever in perpetuating the conspiracy. Thus, the circle is closed as it reaches universities, media outlets and Soros-supported NGOs, for ironically it seems that the disseminators of conspiracy narratives have internalised the basic claim of poststructuralist philosophy – *power belongs to those who say what constitutes knowledge* – and see universities and media outlets as central mechanisms in the machinery of global conspiracy.

Right-wing populist media spheres consider the Frankfurt School's Jewish theoreticians of society and culture led by Herbert Marcuse as the main architects of the "false knowledge" spreading in today's universities and mainstream media. Below, some extracts are given from an article by Tiit Madisson, one of the most notorious political conspiracy theorists in Estonia, that appeared in Rahvuslik Teataja, a publication advocating ultranationalist ideology. In our estimation, these concisely sum up the systemic narrative of cultural Marxism being a decadent ideology that is expressed (usually in less harsh terms) in many right-wing populist media channels (see Ekman 2016; Kasekamp et al. 2019).

> In 1960–1970 many Western universities turned into strongholds of leftist ideology and brainwashing centres that disseminate their ideological views on a "new progressive" way of life, all possible "rights" that are resoundingly classified with human rights (such as having sex with the leg of a stool or a car's exhaust pipe).
>
> [...] According to Marcuse's new revolutionary theory the new revolutionary class is not the proletarians as proposed by his fellow ethnic Marx, but all kinds of ethnic and sexual minorities: the sexual perverts belonging to the LGBT group (that now has received a new, condensated and expanded meaning: LGGBOTTTIQQAAP in which also those into shagging the dead and animals have found their rightful place), the gender neutral set, the extreme left, feminists, those who label themselves antifascists, all possible "refugees" of different races, Islamists, etc. with whose help it is hoped to destroy the societies that are still based on the existing culture, tradition, family and the church.
>
> (Tiit Madisson 2018)

These quotations vividly demonstrate the global perspective characteristic of a system narrative and the logic of the all-inclusive explanation. To summarise the author's ideas, it can be claimed that malevolent and subtle dissemination of a perverted ideology occurs in Western universities, and, by extension, in society as a whole, first and foremost under the aegis of *defending minority rights* and that this has already achieved a relaxation of the natural and traditional norms of morality so that societies are endangered by all possible *minorities* gaining power over the *majority*.

Yet how does all this concern Soros? In Tiit Madisson's words, Soros and "other Jewish bankers" have "set the destruction of nation states and building a multicultural world order as the aim of their activities" (Tiit Madisson 2018). The author indicates in his piece that as early as the 1980s, Soros created a network of Open Societies, which includes the Open Estonia Foundation that was established in 1990 and whose aim is not to support higher education, as is generally presumed, but "understanding of the new and 'correct' ideology and its dissemination", and its ultimate aim is "subversion of the nation states". In addition to this, Soros and his minions have "founded also other subversive networks such as Doctors without Borders and Save the Children" (ibid.).

A conspiracy narrative drawing on a similar motif yet expanding its circle of malignant actors with a global reach up to the leader of the Catholic church can be met in a translation of a Breitbart article published in Uued Uudised, the organ of the Conservative People's Party of Estonia (Vatikani diil … 2018). It bears a telling title: "Vatican's deal with globalists and Soros supporters: A gay agenda and talk of multiculturalism in return for silence surrounding paedophilia". The gist of its contents appears in the following: "Breitbart analyses the latest child abuse scandals of the Catholic church. In the light of this it may become slightly more understandable why the present Pope so ardently praises mass immigration and homosexuality" (ibid). It is remarkable that the sources of danger pointed at in these materials (migrants, Jewish scholars, universities, sexual minorities, etc.) are not perceived as specific active agents, but rather as puppets whom the conspirators need in order to realise their malevolent plans of eradicating traditional values and nation states. Thus, these groups and individuals are mentioned as threatening the *normal* way of life and value climate, but the main guilt and the fully earned status of the puppet master or the grey eminence is attributed to a narrow circle, whom the conspiracy theories call *top globalists, the One World Government* or the *ZOG* (*Zionist Occupation Government*). It is among this set that the right-wing populist conspiracy theories place George Soros.

The main proof that the Jewish billionaire is personally contributing to the dissemination of malignant false knowledge is found in the initiatives funded by the Open Society Foundation that support minority groups and citizen initiatives perceived as threatening by right-wing populists. In addition to this, the Central European University, that has received considerable funding from Soros, prominently figures in such explanations as its Gender Studies programme is seen as a powerhouse of undermining traditional family values and morality space. It was largely due to the conspiracy associations that had become established in the public information space and the pressure from the Hungarian government that the CEU had to transfer a major part of its lectures to Vienna in 2018 (see also Kalmar et al. 2018). The Hungarian government, however, has expressed the opinion that, in principle, the move to Vienna will not change anything: "Up to now Central European University has operated here, it does so now, and we think that it will continue to do so in the future. The relocation to Vienna of the issuing body for its American degrees is simply part of a political ploy" (Walker 2018). It is presumed that the spreading of dangerous ideologies through secret networks and brainwashing will be continued there as such an influencing mechanism has been very effectively established by Soros. In this sense, Soros does not represent an ordinary party-political opponent, he is, to use the words of the Hungarian government spokesman Zoltán Kovács, an insidious *political player*. "He's using his very excessive network of so-called civil organizations, NGOs, to influence in political power. This is a different kind of democracy from what we believe in" (Hume 2018).

An understanding of Soros as a puppet master subtly influencing the sphere of education has been "translated" into the Estonian context as well. An article published in the right-wing populist online media outlet Objektiiv (Maksimov 2019) claims that Estonia's institutions of higher education, particularly the humanities and social studies scholars of Tallinn University, constitute a dangerous propaganda machinery that "enforces its liberal globalist agenda with the help of eager key persons and projects". To corroborate the corruption of Tallinn University, or "Soros's Party school", the piece indicates that several of its Rectors "have been closely connected with the Soros Foundation" and that Estonian universities have been heavily relying on financing from the Open Estonia Foundation during the past 25 years. The author also judges Estonia's Minister of Education as corrupt as she is "an alumna of Central European University that has close ties with Soros's foundations" (ibid).

Also, mainstream media (e.g. professional media enterprises, public media channels) are seen as a sphere of brainwashing conducted by Soros and his supporters in right-wing populist conspiracy theories. In the Estonian right-wing populist information space, Soros's speech at the World Economic Forum in January 2019 gained quite extensive attention. The speech criticised Facebook and Google for their monopolist status and declining of responsibility for the negative results of their activities. An article that appeared in Uued Uudised expressed the opinion that Soros attacked Facebook because of the realisation that it is turning into a discussion forum that offers an alternative to the biased information space of himself and other globalists and that this was frightening him: "After the takeover of Western liberal media by leftist liberal forces it is social media that has largely taken over the role of traditional media and is often guiding resistance to globalism. Apparently, this is what the elderly billionaire who considers himself the centre of the world is afraid of" (Davosis netihiiglaste ... 2018). The idea that mainstream media is biased and submitted to a decadent elite seems to be so strongly established in the interpretative community well versed in system conspiracy theories that it is often referred to as common sense that requires no additional proof, while references to the corrupt media occur very frequently.

Dominant textual strategies

The system narrative of the Soros-led global conspiracy is full of references to the NWO. These appear in the basic lexicon, e.g. in the abundant use of such phrases as *(top) globalists, Soros supporters, cultural Marxists, brainwashing*, etc. Such keywords have a fairly vague reference, due to which they can be used widely and thus they emerge as popular and seem familiar also to interpreters who are only superficially aware of right-wing populist conspiracy theories. The phrases are connected to a clearly pernicious group or their malignant actions and, particularly in the texts in which they appear side by side with such acronyms as NWO or ZOG, can activate the code text of conspiracy theory that merges events and agents that seem to be totally separate for an outside observer into a unified explanation (Madisson 2016b, 201). It is remarkable that combinations of such basic vocabulary guide the Model Reader well-versed in conspiracy theories towards interpretations involving conspiracies, even in cases when the text in question does not explicitly discuss the heinous deeds of secret groups. The specific vocabulary characteristic of conspiracy theories triggers strong associations with conspiracies for members of the interpretative community.

This has immediate connections with intertextual scenarios that have become crystallised in such basic vocabulary. The NWO conspiracy theories became known in the 1990s when Pat Robertson's book *The New World Order* (1991) was published and its descriptions of a global system of evil and the power mechanism of the conspirators moved on both to the fundamentalist anti-establishment information space (e.g. radical-conservative Christians, the extreme right, the radical left) (see Fenster 2008) as well as to various texts of popular culture (e.g. the television series *The X-Files* (1993–2002), the film *Conspiracy Theory* (1997) (Barkun 2003), see Chapter 4 on relating popular musicians with associations with the Illuminati). Today's rightwing populist conspiracy theories refer to these texts as well as secondary texts referencing them (e.g. YouTube videos, writings by Alex Jones or Estonia's best-known conspiracy theorists Jüri Lina and Tiit Madisson). As these texts serve as a pattern, the conspiracy theories we have analysed often contain the ordinary scenario of brainwashing that more broadly refers to the ideas of mind control which presume a complex machinery based on informational and psychological influencing that is capable of paralysing humans' critical thought and, in extreme cases, depriving them of any agency (see Melley 2002).

The syncretistic system narrative connects extremely varied actors and interest groups who are perceived as dangerous but uses relatively clear-cut tactics of ideological hypercoding to legitimise them. In the case of the examples we analyse, one of the tropes that emerges as strategic encoding is that of anti-Semitism that connects Jews who have been active in different time periods and different walks of life (Marxist academics, bankers, Soros's foundations) with obscure global manipulations and moral decline in general. The trope of the corrupt nature of Jews and their secret infiltration of the elite has far-reaching historical roots and can be seen throughout history, e.g. in Hitler's National Socialist slogans. In our earlier work (see Madisson, Ventsel 2018) we have observed its flourishing in Estonia's extreme-right information space.

In addition to conspiring with use, a forceful, and occasionally downright vulgar, rhetorical-stylistic code of sexual taboos has relatively frequently been employed to delegitimise groups who are perceived as opponents from the perspective of the extreme right world view. Various minority groups, immigrants and universities as proponents of cultural Marxist ideology are often represented in the same chains of meaning as child abusers, necrophiliacs, zoophiliacs, etc. As this is a fairly universal code inciting cultural censure, it easily catches the audience's attention and initiates a meaning transfer also to other actors who are presented as connected with the conspiracy. Particularly often, such sexual taboos will be presented side by side with homosexuality, an outlining of a cause-and-effect relationship between an increased social acceptance of the LGBT community and the growth of manifestations of all kinds of sexual perversities and the moral decline of the Western world. Depicting horrible sexual taboos allows for unequivocal illustration of the seriousness of the moral decline.

In the case of the material we analysed, an anti-communist code also emerged that is strongly rooted in both Estonian as well as Hungarian national discourse of memory and identity. For instance, in the Estonian context, communism is clearly related to occupation, deportations, communist party dictatorship, Russification, censorship, etc. and thus functions as a powerful generator of negative associations. Extreme right conspiracy theories do not spell it out that Soros and the funds and universities in his sphere of influence act like communists, but signifiers pointing at communism are often used to describe them: minorities and supporters of a liberal leftist world view are seen as "cultural Marxist" and "the revolutionary class", while Tallinn University is "Soros's party school".

The plurality of the codes described above points at a specificity of the system narrative. Although the Model Reader is being guided towards constructing the conflict with the help of antithetical logic, for instance by attributing the top globalists active in the upper layer of the conspiracy pyramid inhumanly malevolent or even Satanist aims via using the code of sexual taboos (cf. the theory of Pizzagate and Hillary Clinton's purported engagement with a secret network of Satanists and pedophiles), the conflict between value worlds is but rarely expressed as particular events caused by Soros and his stooges. The systemic sabotage on part of the Jewish billionaire and other top globalists is represented as extremely hideous and dangerous, but it is going on in an extremely hidden way through influencing the education and media systems. The conflict on which these conspiracy theories are based can be characterised as being open, agonistic, yet structurally antithetical, as it is presumed that most of the people who have been brainwashed by the Soros set are not aware that they are being influenced by conspirators. A wide-reaching collage is created of explanatory elements (actors, basic vocabulary, ordinary scenarios) that are multi-faceted and all-encompassing (what can be left out from a world view?). They make it possible to create a Model Reader who is capable of spontaneously activating so-called standard modelling schemes (e.g. brainwashing, the conspirators' subtle infiltration of the elite) in different interpretative situations and seeing the big picture of a conspiracy.

Functions

In contrast to political conspiracy narratives, the system narratives telling of malignant manipulation of basic values and social norms do not have as their main aim shaping the perception of the situation and interpretations connected with particular events. Nevertheless, they fulfil an important strategic function that is connected with creating a favourable interpretative context for the receiver of the messages, that keeps the code text of conspiracy theory in communal memory and creates cohesion between different subnarratives. As was outlined in the theoretical part of our book, meaning-making that is based on conspiracy theories is characterised by an extremely high modelling capacity that allows seemingly separate actors and events to be joined together in an explanatory whole and see repeating conspiration patterns behind social developments that are perceived as unpleasant. Such an integrative function was vividly expressed in narratives representing a malevolent dominant system of knowledge. Presuming a far-reaching conspiracy of the left-wing elite led by Soros makes it possible to add into a complex explanation all the agents perceived as dangerous from the point of view an extreme-right world view. Thus, in an all-embracing brainwashing narrative, groups with very different socio-cultural and ideological profiles mingle: professors of Western universities, sexual minorities, feminists, Islamists, migrants who have arrived in Europe as a result of the migration crisis, and anti-fascists. The conspiracy theory made it possible to pass a strongly negative moral judgement on all of them; in one way or another they were seen as collaborating with an inhumanly malevolent elite.

Keeping such narratives in circulation fulfils the function of fixing and freshening of the connections in the communal memory of the interpretative community. Listing other heinous deeds of globalists, Soros supporters or cultural Marxists or adding another reference to the corrupt nature of the NWO system, is not likely to offer the Model Reader aware of conspiracy theories much thrill and joy of discovery, but it is a most effective way of creating a common permutation of typical plot elements and key actors that the members of the interpretative community support between themselves and employ without further explanation in their in-group interactions. If the sender of strategic messages is able to naturalise certain plot turns and characters in the interpretative community, he or she will be able to use them in creating the desired associations when planning his or her future messages. On the one hand, repeating the NWO system conspiracy theory and linking it with different topical political events and actors makes them more significant via the conspiracy (they are not simply problematic actors, but agents of a system of evil), yet on the other hand it increases the significance of the conspiracy theory – it becomes more and more obvious due to its frequent appearance.

A conspiracy narrative speaking of the decadence of the dominant knowledge regime presumes, and at the same time constructs, a Model Reader who is negatively and sceptically disposed towards the mainstream and rather prefers social media and other alternative sources. The Model Author lets him- or herself appear as critical and insightful, someone who establishes an alternative knowledge that is immune to the conspirators' manipulations. The Model Author forcefully opposes the elite and institutions connected with so-called traditional knowledge (universities, professional press, the Pope) and identifies him- or herself as a vernacular authority that has risen from the ranks of the so-called thinking people. Perception of such knowledge and attitudes as arising from the grassroots level functions as a criterion of trustworthiness, their value is expressed not so much in the quality of the claims and the demonstrations, but first and foremost in opposing the mainstream that is suppressing our right-wing populist knowledge. It is remarkable that the Model Author expresses the power position in grip of decadent forces, but at the same time it stresses the vitality of the alternative sphere and its ever-growing social role (Soros is afraid and therefore critical of social media).

Conspiracy narrative of marketing: using associations with Soros in PR

As we pointed out in the beginning of this chapter, the three thematic fields of conspiracy narratives chosen by us are intermingled and in the first analytical chapter we discussed the case of Orbán's poster campaign in which conspiracy theories targeting Soros were disseminated with the aim of political marketing. One of the best-known examples of using the myth of the Jewish billionaire in corporate marketing derives from autumn 2018. Then it became apparent that Facebook, an extremely influential technology giant, had been commissioning contributions from the political consultancy and PR firm Definers, which had a Republican background, that disseminated unsupported claims that Soros was stirring ungrounded dissatisfaction with the enterprise and even organising an anti-Facebook movement (Wong 2018b). At the beginning of 2018, Facebook suffered extensive loss of reputation in connection with the Cambridge Analytica data scandal in which it became apparent that the personal data of millions of individuals was gathered from Facebook profiles without their users' consent and used for political advertising purposes. As Facebook's stock price was falling and the company faced a consumer backlash, it took rather desperate steps to improve its reputation (Frenkel et al. 2018). Hints at Soros's vague behind-the-scenes directions fitted into the context of the PR action as the billionaire had been publicly critical of Facebook, and because theories connected with him were globally so popular that the mere mentioning of Soros's name would immediately provoke conspiracy associations in a rather broad audience.

Dominant textual strategies

Through the PR activities of Definers, a conflict proceeding from antithetical logic was created that represented Facebook as the victim of an unfair and systemic hidden slander campaign. Soros, however, appeared in the ordinary scenario of the puppet master typically connected with him: namely obscure financing schemes and non-profit organisations were hinted at, through which he is supposed to enforce his malignant power ambitions. In the Definers' campaign, these groups were, for example, Freedom from Facebook and Color of Change (see Wong 2018b). Repeating of such meaning-making based on the code text of this conspiracy theory in the case of themes connected with Soros is particularly combustible as it creates a certain equivalence between the narrating situation and earlier cases in which secret manipulations have been hinted at in connection with him. For a target audience who is aware of the basic events of the Soros-themed conspiracy theories (e.g. dissemination of cultural Marxist propaganda in educational establishments, urging mass immigration, organising fake protests, etc.), such concrete suggestions appear to be mutually corroborating one another. Characteristically of the antithetical conflict type, such mirror projection becomes an important shaper of connections that represents the spheres of influence both of the own and the adversary as powerful, while the former is perceived as an embodiment of fairness and the latter that of corruption. The conspiracy theories discussed on the one hand amplify the idea that Soros's machinations are per-petually behind questions concerning communal life, while, on the other hand, they suggest that Facebook is suffering from persecution by an extremely dangerous and influential adversary. As in these conspiracy narratives the damage caused by Soros's secret machinations is represented as being of a short duration and relatively easily localised, such stories do not so much demonstrate the easy manipulability of the Internet giant as they add to the certainty of Facebook being an extremely weighty enterprise both socially as well as politically. The logic of conspiracy theories as a rule does not connect a powerful supervillain with acting against small-scale adversaries but sees Soros's activity as directed against the most effective targets in a clear and calibrated manner.

When, in the autumn of 2018, the media started to demand that Zuckerberg should comment on such anti-Semitic PR activities, he claimed: "I didn't know of Facebook ties to firm that attacked George Soros" (Wong 2018c). The Internet giant quickly ended cooperation with Definers, and this is probably one of the reasons why the references to Soros were not developed into versatile subconflicts and subtopics. As an important rhetorical encoding, it can be suggested that the Model Author poses as a force that sets a high value to the qualities of being sci-entific and proof-based. Namely, both Facebook and Definers presented reaching the hidden traces of Soros as resulting from opposition research. Such encoding is directed at the Model Reader for whom references to science add authority and weight to claims. As a rule, such references activate connotations with thoroughness, neutrality and controllability of knowledge and move such content from the discursive sphere of speculations, opinions and political debates of the day. In summer 2018, Definers shared with media a research document linking Soros with a broad anti-Facebook movement (Frenkel et al. 2018). Definers suggested that the media should also conduct a more thorough study of the links between Soros's family and the movements that were members of Freedom from

Facebook, such as Color of Change, as well as a progressive group founded by Soros's son (Frenkel et al. 2018, Wong 2018b). As was mentioned above, such sowing of suspicion and mentioning of connections, while the construction of more thorough links was left to the receiver of information, is fairly typical of today's conspiracy narratives. Strategic narrators invite their Model Readers (in this case, journalists) to conduct independent research work. Simultaneously, they give them firm directions as regards the results that might be reached as result of such search for connections and following of the code text present in the communal memory – to the revelation of yet another machination of the Jewish billionaire and his stooges.

Conspiracy narrative of marketing: deliberate connection of branded products with conspiracies

In order to illustrate the phenomenon of employing conspiracy theories in marketing more broadly, we decided to make a little detour from the narratives connected with Soros. Namely, we have not yet come across examples of PR strategists making connections between the products or brands they are advertising and conspiracy associations related to Soros. At the same time, such use of conspiracy theories is a noticeable trend in today's attention economy; for instance, in 2018 the humorous advertising campaign of Denver Airport that was saturated with hints at conspiracies caused much excitement and public reactions (see Williams 2018; Wolfson 2018). Conspiracy theories are usually intriguing and evoke a mysterious atmosphere that attracts the audience's heightened attention, and often also their willingness to participate actively in the process of exposing the conspiracy. The marketing component of messages that have been spiced with thrilling conspiracy details reaches the addressees through an interpretation game and helps to attach a certain dose of "coolness" to the products that are being advertised. It is important to note that before unleashing marketing conspiracy narratives the coolhunters of PR companies search the social media groups and forums that mediate the most preposterous conspiracy theories and rumours and, on this basis, distil both the emerging trends for the plot twists and the freshest sensational actors (Karlova, Fisher 2013, 13). In the next phase, conspiracy narratives are created that blend particular brands and recognisable conspiracy codes, and at times also codes that are cryptic for broader audiences that make it possible to achieve an effect of maximum novelty and intrigue. We are treating the latter as a special case of stylistic encoding that aims to cultivate thrill and mystery. Thereafter, these are emitted onto platforms of various participant media. Such marketing content can parody a conspiracy theory and generate a feeling of humour and superiority in media consumers. However, the tactic of shocking or frightening the audience that maintains a permanent atmosphere of interest and tension can also be chosen.

Conspiracy narratives have been applied rather vigorously in promoting the personal brands of such stars connected with the American music industry such as Madonna, Jay Z, Beyoncé, Lady Gaga, Rihanna, Kanye West and others (Stæhr 2014). Such discourse achieved peak popularity in the middle of 2010, flourishing primarily on social media (Facebook, YouTube) under the umbrella label of Illuminati Gossip. The music videos, song lyrics, public appearances and social media profiles are full of basic vocabulary of Illuminati and NWO conspiracy theories, such as the all-seeing eye; pyramids and triangles; pentagrams; occasional references to Satan as being in league with the conspirators, e.g. a goat's head and horns; and numeric symbols connected with Satan such as *666, 13*. Sometimes also the visual codes of reptile theories (vertical pupils, lacking white of the eye, peculiar (rough, flaky) skin texture, glowing, lack of mimics, etc.) are introduced. Many conspiracy codes have been borrowed from Christian demonology and they create intertextual connections with both historical as well as contemporary representations of Satan, as well as such works of the popular conspiracy theorist David Icke as *The Biggest Secret: The Book That Will Change the World* (1999) and *Infinite Love Is the Only Truth: Everything Else Is Illusion* (2005), or other videos of pop stars that contain strong references to conspiracies. Such conspiracy codes presume a Model Reader who is willing to do interpretative detective work. For such a reader, hints at conspiracy theories can be a source of much excitement and speculations: e.g. considering if the stars are mutually connected by the conspiracy and form a secret network, as well as the temptation to follow the traces of conspiracy together with the other "initiated", as it were, and share the newest findings of signs of conspiracy.

Dominant textual strategies

The marketing discourse evoking associations with the Illuminati creates a Model Reader whose interpretative activities are guided by the active search for, and discovery of, signs of conspiracy. It is important that these signs occur constantly and with a sufficient frequency so that a desire might emerge in the audience to study them independently and attempt to find more of them. As was mentioned above, one of the characteristics of the meaning-making in conspiracy theories is unrestricted meaning-making or strong enthusiasm for interpretations whose most important component is the presumption that the interpreter has access to certain signs left behind by a conspiracy. For instance, Lady Gaga's fans who have recognised obvious hints at Satan and the Illuminati in her songs have started to look for them in her interviews, lapses of the tongue, playing her music backwards, numerology connected with her performances and dates of life, etc.; that is, in places where the senders of strategic marketing messages have not been able to plant them. So, it is comparatively typical that the "evidence" of a conspiracy is considered all the more valuable, the more hidden or indirect it is.

The Model Author who appeals to references at the Illuminati is well versed in the main plots of conspiracy theories and the trending themes, presuming also knowledge and appreciation of popular conspiracy codes on the part of the audience. The latter includes the basic conflict between Good and Evil and the presumption that a large number of people allow a conspiracy network to rule over them due to their cluelessness and ignorance, and to broaden their evil grip. Hollywood films as well as the video game industry have naturalised an ordinary scenario of the conspiracy theorist hero that creates an opposition of forces that are corrupt through and through and may even be in league with Satan, with a few protagonists who can see through the former's manipulations. Pop stars are represented as in service of the top levels of conspiracy pyramids; occasionally, conspiracy narratives bring out brainwashing, or corrupting the audience with their amoral messages and evoking an interest in dark forces as their main task. The ordinary scenario also prescribes that those exposing conspiracies are initially ridiculed and labelled as paranoid but, in the end, they manage to find sufficient evidence and open the eyes of the public or foil the villainous manipulations in another way.

On the other hand, it is important to note that in conspiracy theories connected with pop stars the strategically constructed conflict is based on a model that is in principle different from that which can be seen in the case of conspiracy theories concerned with the realm of politics that were explained in an earlier subchapter. These described conspirators as essentially evil puppet masters who should be eradicated from society together with their conspiracy, while the Illuminati Gossip represents potential conspirators in a more ambivalent and even more positive light. The stars do not use such a strategy of self-branding in order to become hated anti-heroes but in order to attract attention and blend a share of power and mystery into their image. Conspiracy narratives that are strategically disseminated do not, as a rule, depict pop stars as unambiguously evil villains, but they are positioned as, in a way, victims of the puppet masters who may have an important role in implementing the wicked plans, but are not their primary initiators. Through the celebrities, the connection with conspiracy occasionally turns into a downright glamorous depravity. For instance, it has been noted that teenage fans consciously imitate the hand signs containing references to pop star conspiracies (such as forming triangles with thumbs and index fingers) and other such visual codes in communicating with their peers (Stæhr 2014), as they can so demonstrate a certain unitedness with their idols, while, in addition to this, such connections with conspiracies seem provocative and forbidden, which signifies coolness in the eyes of many teenagers. Such conspiracy narratives attempt to activate a Model Reader for whom pop stars are not merely icons of a superficial media industry but serve as important links to a secret power network controlling the world.

In addition to this, the image creation of stars is accompanied by a constant questioning of the existence of the conspiracy. As is characteristic of conspiracy theories spreading in contemporary web environments, articles in tabloid newspapers and the stars' marketing messages invite the interpreters to revise the "evidence" and draw their own conclusions as refers to the secret network. As regards conspiracy theories concerning pop stars, strategic ambivalence is often advocated – a certain as-if position in which it remains open whether the conspiracy really exists or whether it is merely a part of the fictional character world. Perceiving such an ambivalent boundary between the, as-it-were, I-position of the narrator and the enacted character perspective is an ordinary part of the interpretative experience of the audience growing up among the micro-celebrities of social media (Abidin 2018). For instance, the storytelling of practices of YouTubers involves, as a typical device, that the performers develop several "characters" or "actors" from whose points of view they deliver their messages. Occasionally, transitions between characters and the I-voice of the micro-celebrity are clearly marked, yet at times they are not. A strategy employed by pop stars who use conspiracy theories for self-promotion is making conspiracy references more ambiguous by producing a flood of conspiracy signs. Thus, they constantly, and at times jocularly, use the code of the all-seeing eye in their public appearances or social media postings or make continuous references to the intertextual NWO scenario. An audience aware of the code text of the conspiracy theory may find such public activity widely reflected in tabloids suspicious, as a basic component of the code text of conspiracy narratives – secrecy – is strongly compromised in such representations.

Functions

Examples introduced in this chapter demonstrated that strategic conspiracy theories spread with marketing purposes can fulfil various functions, while often a broader creation of the image of *us* has merged with more particular communicative aims. The Soros hints launched in the PR collaboration of Facebook and Definers served the classic rhetorical aim – projecting a set of problems on a single scapegoat. The main function of such communication was to activate conspiracy stereotypes connected with Soros and delegitimise criticism of Facebook made by this allegedly wicked person. There was an attempt to create a feeling of doubt and confusion that would corroborate that something suspicious was afoot in the financing of counter-Facebook movements, so that even if no concrete evidence could be produced, it was still worth approaching the theme through a sceptical filter. The narratives disseminated by Definers also involved the subnarrative of attributing the image of a positive, unjustly persecuted active agent to Facebook.

The main aim of the marketing discourse cultivating associations with the pop star conspiracy is to cultivate in the audience a general excitement and interpretative enthusiasm in connection with certain personal brands. Virally spreading conspiracy threads has a high value in the contemporary attention economy, as they are equally useful to click-hungry tabloids as well as to stars who need a permanent presence in the media spectacle to maintain their popularity. Audience attention is admittedly a limited resource and, as was demonstrated above, the partly funny, yet partly extremely alarming, infotainment-style conspiracy theories that involve famous (anti-)heroes efficiently attract that attention. A secondary function of such conspiracy theories is creating a heroic self-description in the target audience. As the conspirators are depicted as acting hidden from the audience, those aware of conspiracy theories can position themselves as a privileged perceptive minority in the know. The marketing discourse saturated with references to conspiracies offers the target audience the possibilities of a certain flattering of the ego in addition to excitement – doing what teenagers would want to do anyway, that is, consuming popular culture they can also contribute to playfully exposing hidden/forbidden knowledge and invite others to open their eyes. What is undoubtedly important about the marketing strategy relying on conspiracy theories is the aspect of community creation: members of an active audience like to share the results of their interpretative detective work with others. Belonging to a wicked secret network of stars can be a fascinating shared subject and can serve as the foundation of a specific niche of fandom.

Notes

1 A psychoanalytical approach to text generation in semiotics has been offered by Julia Kristeva (1969) who differentiates between the genotext and the fenotext and Roland Barthes (1980) who discusses the differentiation between the concepts of the work and the text.

2 Propastop is a blog of volunteers from the Estonian Defence League. It uses media monitoring and data analysis for comprehending disinformation campaigns that target Estonia. Propastop's goal is to increase public awareness of the Kremlin's disinformation campaigns and promote critical media literacy.

3 Fidesz, or the Hungarian Civic Alliance, has been the main political party in power in Hungary starting from 2010, and has been led by the current Prime Minister Viktor Orbán through those years. The party is known for its anti-immigration, Eurosceptical and populist right-wing politics.

4 EUvsDisinfo is the flagship project of the European External Action Service's East StratCom Task Force. It was established in 2015 to better forecast, address and respond to the Russian Federation's ongoing disinformation campaigns affecting the European Union, its Member States, and countries in the shared neighbourhood.

5 The quotation is a loose translation from a television programme *60 Minutes* on the channel Rossiya 1 (21 June 2019), where he was an invited guest as an expert on the politics of the Middle East and the Caucasus (24:10–24:39).

6 Protests in Georgia started on the night of 21 June; discontent in Georgia was provoked by the visit of a Russian delegation to Tbilisi to participate in the Inter-Parliamentary Assembly of Orthodoxy.

7 Starting from 2014, hostilities are continuing in Ukraine between the separatist parts of Eastern Ukraine (Lugatsk, Donetsk) and the central power led from Kiev. For Ukraine and the West, one of the parties represented in the conflict is Russia who provides support to the separatists. Russia has been denying its activities there, which is why pro-Kremlin information channels represent the conflict as a civil war. Georgia saw a civil war in 1991–1994.

8 What is hinted at is the conflict in Nagorno-Karabakh between the Azerbaijani and the Armenians living in South Caucasus. The conflict, with long-lasting historical and cultural roots, escalated during the *perestroika* years in the Soviet Union (1987–1988) and burst out in hostilities between Armenia and Azerbaijan in 1991–1994 for the control of Nagorno-Karabakh and some surrounding regions. Today, the Republic of Artsakh (that declared independence on 2 September 1991) is a disputed territory in Nagorno-Karabakh and a continuous source of conflict in the relations between

Azerbaijan and Armenia, as after the ceasefire in the war of Nagorno-Karabakh the Armenian-majority Republic of Artsakh controls a part of the Azerbaijani territory.

9 The Conservative People's Party of Estonia (EKRE) is a national-conservative and right-wing populist political party in Estonia. Since 2013, the leader of the party has been Mart Helme (Estonian Minister for the Interior starting from 29 April 2019), among its leading figures is also his son Martin Helme (Minister of Finance starting from 29 April 2019).

10 In Romanian political rhetoric, the governing party has also employed Soros-themed conspiracy theories to undermine the reputation of its opponents. First and foremost, he has been accused of financing various demonstrations. The accusation that Soros paid for the protests against Donald Trump, after the latter had won the US presidency, only adds to the picture of the so-called bleak future of Eastern European nations in the age of globalisation. Possibly for the first time, a conspiracy theory that originated in this part of the world became common knowledge in the West (Nazaryan 2017). Likewise, Soros serves as the embodiment of both Jewish and Hungarian conspiracy theories in Romanian far-right politics (Colăcel, Pintilescu 2017, 35).

4 The main meaning-making mechanisms of strategic conspiracy narratives

The previous chapter concentrated on the dominant textual strategies via which the Model Reader and the Model Author of conspiracy narratives are created. The function of textual strategies is to establish particular interpretative links in the audience via which readers can be directed towards goals that are being aspired to, using the narrative. Often such strategic communication functions through shaping the interpretative community's collective identity or undermining its opponents' legitimacy. In the following we shall concentrate on the discursive devices that help some conspiracy theories to have a greater potential to affect the interpreters' interpretations and values, as they attract attention and achieve viral spread.

Conspiracy theories as a trigger of affective communication

Several authors have pointed out that social media has become the main place of spreading and discussing conspiracy theories (Ballinger 2011, 3; Bergmann 2018, 154). One of the reasons for such a tendency consists in the socio-technical affordances of social media that allows for the formation of audiences on an unprecedented temporal (very fast), spatial (geographically dispersed) and affective (strong, mobilising sentiment) scale (Tiidenberg, Siibak 2018, 4). Due to the affordances, some ways of behaviour or application are more convenient and obvious, and thus likelier to occur on social media than others (Tiidenberg 2017, 21). The popularity of reactions and functions of copying and sharing is connected with the discussion space on social media becoming less reliant on argument and more affect-based, while amplification of the feelings of being connected and involved as well as experiencing texts together have an unprecedented role. As indicated in the subchapter "Affective narrating practices and affective communities", an expression of affective communal experience is particularly likely to occur on social media in times of crises, catastrophes and conflicts, that is, in cases in which social media is used to express collective concern and irritation (Papacharissi 2014). As the code-textual centre of conspiracy theory is based on an unsolvable conflict and the presence of a malevolent actor, strategic conspiracy narratives are often constructed upon textual devices that provoke affective reactions, such as fear and irritation.

Scholars of strategic narratives Alister Miskimmon and Ben O'Loughlin (2019, 274) point out that affective loaded-ness is to be considered in the analysis of narratives, as the feelings of actors constitute an important component of storyworlds, they have an important role in shaping the interpreters' perception of the situation and their decisions regarding behaviour. At the same time, it is admitted that the mechanisms of this kind of meaning-making need more academic study in the context of strategic narratives (Miskimmon et al. 2017, 317). Our approach suggests that the metalanguage of cultural semiotics can be fruitfully applied not only to the content of "what" is articulated, but also to "how" it is articulated.

What is affective semiosis?

According to cultural theorist Lawrence Grossberg, affect "is articulated and disarticulated — there are affective lines of articulation and affective lines of flight— through social struggles over its structure" (1992, 82). It means that affect is closely related with meaning-making processes.

Semiotic cultural psychologists Sergio Salvatore and Maria F. Freda describe the semiotic standpoint that "looks at affect not merely as a reactive embodied activation but as the use of this activation as a basic form of meaning, that is as the first interpretant motivated in the interpreter's mind, in turn triggering further interpreting signs. For this reason, affect is to be considered in terms of process rather than of state – affect then, as *affective semiosis* (2011, 122). According to semiotic cultural psychologist Jaan Valsiner, who relies primarily on Peirce's tradition of semiotics, first introduced the term affective semiosis, "*Affect* (affective phenomena) is here defined as the common descriptive term that subsumes both feelings (as felt by the person) and emotions (as those are expressed, recognized, and described in language terms)" (Valsiner, 2007). It means these are collectively shared and collectively constructed. Feelings are inherently ambiguous while *emotions* are discrete (point-like) categories that are accessible for labelling, discursive operations, and abstraction/generalisation. They are "differentiated, articulated and hierarchically integrated" (Branco, Valsiner 2010, 243).

This kind of affective meaning-making expresses a collective intuitive recognition that some elements or signs of a strategic narrative are highly relevant, but the interpreter does not divide them into different logical-discrete structures. These signs firstly evoke an emotional reaction in the audience, the feeling of primary – either positive or negative – identification. Conspiracy theories, especially in social media communication, often do not explicitly outline the relations between various subnarratives of conspiracies referred to, but rather function as open-ended (and sometimes even controversial) sets of stories (see the subchapter "Studying conspiracy theories spreading on the Internet"). The interpreter can navigate through various plot fragments and draw his/her own conclusions about causalities (Knight 2008, Soukup 2008). Those kinds of discourses are often driven by affective meaning-making that is based on a rough and approximate type of relations. In order to guide the interpretation paths of the targeted audience in a direction suitable for the creator of the narrative, the Model Reader constructed in a strategic conspiracy narrative has to contain signs, text excerpts, visuals, etc. that carry an emotional load for the audience (in more detail, see the subchapter "Dominant textual strategies of transmedia story-telling"). These trigger affective semiosis that guides the reader towards making associative links between various subnarratives and plot fragments. It is important to note that this kind of affective dimension is particularly strong in the case of topics that resonate with the negative emotions of the audience, especially if they coincide with loss of happiness (Ahmed 2010) or "fears and anxieties about the future" (Grusin 2010, 46).

Dominant textual strategies of affective semiosis

Several strategic conspiracy narratives represented in the previous chapter were constructed with a dominant that triggers affective semiosis. On the one hand, this is to be expected, as conspiracy theories rely on a conflict at their centre, that can be represented as existentially more or less destructive. It is particularly true in the conflicts in conspiracy narratives of political and alternative know-ledge that have been constructed as an antithesis between *us* and *them* and in which the adversaries are depicted as actually endangering the existence of conspiracy theorists. As regards textual strategies, these conspiracy narratives relied on the basic structure of the conspiracy narrative in which Soros and his minions were depicted as organisers of real military conflicts. The Estonian radical right-wing news and opinion portal Uued Uudised writes:

> The further we move into the East, the more evil Soros's intentions become. In Ukraine his establishments considerably contributed to the revolutions of 2004 and 2014 and thus to political instability. [...] Leaked e-mail messages demonstrate that Soros has been issuing direct orders to the new government of Ukraine. [...] Also elsewhere in Central and Eastern Europe we can see Soros and the Open Society Institute provoking unrest and instigating wars. They openly participated in Georgia's Revolution of the Roses in 2003 as well as in Serbia's "Bulldozer revolution" in 2000.
>
> (George Soros ... 2016)

One of functions of the use of the war scenario is discursive provocation of feelings of danger. Thus, the audience can activate war-linked meanings in a situation that lacks real characteristics of (empirical) war. As pointed out by the theoretician of fear Frank Furedi, the values, attitudes and expectations of the community provide a cultural context to the expression of personal fears (2019, 13), which means, all in all, that the strategic success of affect-based communication depends on which cultural devices can be used as a source of inspiration (Furedi 2019, 163). In the above example, such a cultural device appears in the form of textual strategical analogies with countries (Ukraine, Georgia) in which real bloody conflicts have taken place that have been widely reported in Estonian media. The aim of the strategic author is to trigger affective semiosis based on emotional attitudes of the audience via signs the audience considers as sensitive.

From a semiotic point of view, the connection between affective semiosis and the discourse of fear can be explained by the suggestion of semiotician of culture Mihhail Lotman, according to whom, from the perspective of semiotics, fear can be treated as a reaction to sign-mediated danger (2007, 208). This means that fear is not just a reaction to a particular event or object itself, but an interpretation of various anticipatory signs or phenomena as terrifying and dangerous (ibid.). In the case of successful strategic communication one of the forces triggering creation of connections in the audience is the context of fear shaped by the war scenario. Such creation of connections is based on affective semiosis in which signs pointing at conspiracy (e.g. secret correspondence between Soros and the *new* government of Ukraine) are perceived by the audience as signs of a potential devastating war. Signs triggering affective semiosis are used to guide the Model Reader towards interpreting signs and subplots presented in the narrative as evidence of the existence of the Soros plot, "as the first interpretant motivated in the interpreter's mind, in turn triggering further interpreting signs" (Salvatore, Freda 2011, 122). The article in Uued Uudised (George Soros ... 2016) referred to above is connected with an analogous future scenario of a war catastrophe and Soros's many other enterprises, such as initiating migration streams, supporting various non-profit organisations, etc.

Conspiracy narratives of alternative knowledge analysed in this book constructed conflicts primarily as a clash of world views or civilisations whose results were depicted as fatal for the community threatened by the conspirators. Soros's direct guilt and malevolence was seen not in triggering particular military conflicts, but in the covert destabilisation of societies, "destroying nation states, constructing a multicultural world order and establishing the New World Order" (Tiit Madisson 2018). Undermining such value systems and discursive mediation of the emotion of fear is often connected with moral norms. The so-called moralisation of fears enables the strategic actors to present the problems and dangers symbolically, lending properties of morals to problems that could otherwise be considered rather insignificant practical things (Furedi 2019, 140). The analysis presented in the previous chapter showed that the opponent's (liberal) ideology was represented as moral (sexual) abnormality, as references to paedophilia, zoophilia, fratricide, etc. were employed to give expression to fear and provoke emotional resonance and affective reactions in the audience. Such references with their relatively fixed emotional and value-related meanings should trigger affective semiosis in the Model Reader, first calling forth in the audience a negative emotional reaction, a certain interpretative background that will also guide the readers' future interpretative paths. The same moralising device appears in the conspiracy narratives that started to spread in the autumn of 2019, in which Soros was accused of the devious and malevolent exploitation of Greta Thunberg, who was portrayed as merely a child suffering from Asperger syndrome (Grey Ellis 2019).

On the other hand, as indicated by several authors, affective semiosis can also be triggered by the opposite of fear – a connection with happiness (Ahmed 2010). These usually appear together; discursively they are represented either more or less explicitly. In narratives of ideological conflict analysed in the previous chapter, the potential trigger of affective semiosis in the Model Reader could be found in a discourse that represented an idealised and harmonious picture of the world. In several examples, in addition to listing Soros's activities, the characteristics of such a world that corresponds to the so-called natural order of things according to conspiracy theorists are listed, e.g. an understanding of the state as monoethnic, heterosexual, containing reverence of patriarchal values and so-called Christian family traditions, large families of children, etc. According to cultural theorist Skip Willman, "conspiracy theories presuppose a fallen society, whose failure constitutes itself as a harmonious whole and must be explained; the conspiratorial narrative resurrects the possibility of society even as it traces its demise through the agency of hidden forces" (2000, 28). For the conspiracy theorists, the figure of the enemy (conspirator) signifies a sharp gap between their ideological representation of a harmonious society – the state of happiness – and the actual experience of society, which cannot be grasped within their cognitive frames in other ways. Agents or enemies from the outside (conspirators) "enable conspiracy theorists to explain social conflicts and devi-ations from ideal communal life and are thus needed for creating a meaningfully coherent world" (Ventsel 2016a, 317). Thus, affective meaning-making also functions as a reference to an ideal state of happiness that is represented as endangered in conspiracy theories.

In articulating social fears, it should be noted that the semiosis of fear is oriented towards looking for a sign expression necessary for communicating a subjective feeling of fear. This is the reason why signification mechanisms of fear are vague and ambivalent in their nature (M Lotman 2007, 151–152) or are based on continuous meaning-making that generates homomorphic resemblance and identification between different elements. Soros's conspiracy theory as a code text constructing the adversary, connects different goal-oriented activities between which a researcher could hardly find a rational part in common. What is the connection between migration streams directed against the US, aiding the opposition forces in Armenia, the Swedish schoolgirl Greta Thunberg and Soros? In the affective semiosis triggered in the Model Reader they are united by Soros as a common enemy, whose hidden aims are perceived as equally frightening and endangering the idea of happiness cherished by conspiracy theorists.

Function of affective semiosis

In strategic communication, affective semiosis fulfils several interconnected aims. Many researchers have pointed out that an emphasis on fear is often used as a tactic to draw attention to a problem in the superabundance of general information on social media and to mobilise people into action (Altheide 2002; Furedi 2019, 111; Nissen 2015; Marwick, Lewis 2017; Swimelar 2018). In this context, fear also appears as an essential discursive means for legitimation of political decisions (Wodak 2015). In the case of the Soros-themed conspiracy narratives analysed in this book, we can see the functions manifested with varying intensity. As a generalisation it can be claimed that what is dominant in the conspiracy narratives of marketing is the attention-grabbing function together with entertainment-flavoured sharing and the joy of further advancing development of the stories. In conspiracy narratives with the dominant of presenting a political adversary or a conflict of world views, textual strategies connected with fear and the transience of happiness, function as triggers of affective semiosis in which attention grabbing and the creating of cohesion between the interpretation paths of the Model Reader are strongly connected with identity creation in targeted interpretative communities.

From the point of view of identity creation, affective semiosis fulfils the function of phatic communication that is primarily expressed in confirming the communion belonging of those engaged in communication (see the subchapter "Conspiracy theories as sources of communion cohesion"). In many ways, phatic communication functions due to the repeating of signs and subplots most significant from the point of view of the value worlds of the interpretative community. The informative novelty of such signs is of secondary importance for the audience, as they are already known and will not be questioned, but their use reasserts the dimension shared by the community. Such affective signs that invite quick identification can be either negatively loaded, i.e. we are against them (hints at child abuse), or bear a positive load, i.e. we are for them (hints at an established understanding of an ideal monoethnic nation state).

On the other hand, affective semiosis can be employed in shaping communities. Here we can speak of a novel logic of community formation which results, first, in the instability and temporary nature of social media groups, and second, in the reduction of complex socio-political issues to a stark yes/no alternative. These new forms of community (see "affective public" in Papacharissi 2014) are characterised by connective action – based on large-scale self-organised, personal content sharing, fluid and weak-tied networks – as opposed to collective action, which is defined by formal organisational control, stronger commitment and collective identity framing (Bennett, Segerberg 2012). In conspiracy narratives such polarisation is manifested in the case of the antithetical conflict type, in which the Model Reader in principle recognises only "yes/no" answers in their primary interpretation of the world. As we indicated in the subchapter "Antithetical and agonistic modelling of conflict", such meaning-making is characteristic of a self-enclosed system that avoids external influences (Lotman, Uspenskij 1978, 220). In this context, deliberation and solving of the conflict through dialogue and argumentation becomes increasingly more difficult, being replaced by affective reactions that signal either "for" or "against". A strategic aim of employing signs triggering affective semiosis is to offer a primary opportunity of identification based on the audience's emotional reactions, which are characterised by connective action-based networks. If such primary affective audiences have been created, this can be used later to achieve more strategic aims. This presumes the generation of more nuanced stories that contain clearer perspectives for the future and action programmes for the audience (see the following subchapter "Transmedial strategic conspiracy narratives") in which connective action-based networks are shaped into collective action-based networks.

Transmedial strategic conspiracy narratives

One of the central challenges in studying strategic narratives is taking into consideration today's hybrid media ecology and its meaning-making trends. Strategic storytelling occurs simultaneously across different platforms and various official spokespersons, social media influencers as well as ordinary users who interact with these stories, make their more or less conscious contributions into the mediation of the narrative. If strategic communication "is marked today by a proliferation of visual, viral content, it is not enough to make assumptions about what idea or narrative it conveys or what it means to policy elites or publics" (Miskimmon et al. 2017, 14). The aim of this subchapter is to offer a brief summary of the remarks made in earlier academic research about strategic storytelling practices embracing different modalities and platforms, and to explain how meaning-making based on the code text of conspiracy theory becomes adapted to such a mode of storytelling. In the second half of the subchapter we explain the logic of the functioning of textual devices used in transmedial storytelling proceeding from the frameworks of cultural semiotics and give some examples to illustrate how the Soros-themed conspiracy narrative has been spreading in different parts of the Estonian right-wing populist information space, which nevertheless are interconnected via references.

Strategic transmedia storytelling and call for immersive experience

Studies that concentrate on multimodal strategic narratives mostly spreading on social media that actively involve the audience have often found that such narrating practices can best be conceptualised as transmedial (Freeman 2016; von Stackelberg, Jones 2014; Monaci 2017; Wiggins 2017) or cross-medial storytelling[1] (Nissen 2015; Jenkins 2011). As a rule, such work proceeds from the definition by Jenkins according to which transmedial storytelling is understood as a "process where integral elements of a fiction get dispersed systematically across multiple delivery channels for the purpose of creating a unified and coordinated entertainment experience. Ideally, each medium makes its own unique contribution to the unfolding of the story." Although in comparison with transmedia projects produced by the contemporary entertainment industry (e.g. the development of the Batman storyworld as mediated by content created in comics, film, series, animation and social media fanfiction), the unfolding of non-fictional transmedia narratives is considerably more dispersed and unpredictable, it still shares a large communal part in its main textual strategies and discursive effects (Freeman 2016, 95). Transmedia narratives are considered very effective in disseminating strategic messages, as they often blend topical information, entertainment and story points furthering the agenda of a particular actor, which is why the audience consuming them does not feel that they are being induced to believe someone's message, but rather the unfolding of such a story is perceived as an exciting, captivating experience (von Stackelberg, Jones 2014, 61).

Studies focusing on transmedia storytelling emphasise that for storytelling to be successful there must be sufficient redundancy between story entries and information fragments presented on different platforms for the audience to be able to interconnect these, and for them to end up "eventually creating a cohesive mental whole, a coherent storyworld" (Ojamaa, Torop 2015, 62). Transmedia storytelling can only function when the same actor has poured several bits of the story, each bit supporting one another, onto the Internet. In order to achieve this, in entries of strategic transmedia narratives numerous interconnecting thematic references and hyperlinks to content presented on other platforms are used (Nissen 2015). An important role in achieving cohesion between different entries is played by the consistent repetition of invariant elements of the narrative (e.g. the basic conflict, actors, the setting) (see Ojamaa, Torop 2015, 62). Such repetitions can be comprehensive looks at earlier representations or laconic and implicit hints that are restricted to mere mentioning of characters and key events and phrases of the basic vocabulary characteristic of some stories. Sara Monaci who has studied the transmedia strategic narratives of the Islamic state, has remarked that in creating cohesion, an important role is played by repetition and redundancy on the story's level of expression, for instance, by constantly employing the same iconic visuals[2] and colour scheme, or the same (narrator's) voice or background sounds (Monaci 2017, 2848). Also, cohesion is created by continually employed tropes and intertextual references; for instance, the Islamic State integrated into its messages verses from the Quran to add solemnity and authority to them (Monaci 2017, 2854–2855). In addition, creating narrative cohesion with the help of elements repeated in different performances, which iterate certain meaning relationships in different sign systems, makes it possible to accept them effectively and establish them in the communal memory of the interpretative community and thus increase their meaningfulness (Ojamaa, Torop 2015, 62).

Despite repetitions occurring on the levels of the story's basic elements and of rhetoric having a crucial function in transmedia narrations, it is at least as important that narrative entries presented on different platforms should contain new elements that enrich the storyworld (see e.g. Evans 2011, 27). In the case of strategic narratives, such an innovative added value can be expressed as offering a new emotional/aesthetic nuance of experience (e.g. visualisation of the action or setting, emotional depiction of characters) or an additive comprehension of the conflict (e.g. introducing a factor explaining the basic events) (see Monaci 2017, 2854). Narrative entries that offer new levels of insight and knowledge about the storyworld help maintain interest on the part of members of the audience and thus guarantee their loyalty to the theme (Nissen 2015, 42).

Often one of the aims of the creators of strategic narratives is to create so strong a resonance in the social media audience that its members will consent to repeat its main strategic message in their own social media threads and so start enriching its storyworld with their remarks and personal micro-stories (see Nissen 2015, Monaci 2017). Such meaning-making by users adds vitality and vernacular authority to strategic narratives, which is one of the most important criteria of credibility in social media communication. Thomas Elkjær Nissen has indicated in connection with user-generated content that although strategic narratives have been put into circulation on social media that have been constructed according to systemic target group analysis, it is impossible for the strategic actor or sender to keep the contribution of the active audience under control (Nissen 2015, 41–42). However, the strategic disseminators of transmedia narratives employ certain devices in order to keep the audience-generated content broadly from conflicting with the main meaning relations (the nature of the groups of the victims and the perpetrators, the basic events of the conflict, the future scenarios) that constitute the treatment of the conflict represented in the strategic narrative, or versions containing major deviations, from obtaining a dominant position in the interpretative community. Such instances of discord can be dissolved to a degree by users who have obtained the status of opinion leaders in interpretative communities, e.g. they can repeat the basic relationships of the strategic narrative and question the compromising versions of the story and their disseminators. A fairly typical practice is via flooding concrete discussion environments (with the help of robot networks or sock puppets) with contents repeating the strategic narrative (see the device *structure* and *push*, Nissen 2015, 43).

In the case of the reception mediated by different platforms, authors and narrative media, strong affective reactions, how engaging it is and playfulness are often foregrounded. Senders of strategic narratives have to create messages perceived as sufficiently exciting, intriguing and urgent for the receivers to develop an enthusiasm for interpretation that might motivate them to move between platforms and elaborate the mental map of their storyworld in the light of additional information. Several authors (von Stackelberg, Jones 2014; Wiggins 2017) have described the reception of effective transmedia narratives as an immersive experience in which the storyworld holds such an interest for interpreters that bits of information that can be linked with the narrative in any manner are adopted quickly and in a way that is comparatively devoid of criticism, and integrated creatively in the general meaning relations of the narrative (see Murray 1997, 110). It is in connection with this circumstance that transmedia narratives allow efficient merging of facts and fiction, real and fabricated events, and hide lapses in logic, dissonance and information gaps that would be considerably more noticeable in the case of a more linear style of narration (cf. written narratives) (von Stackelberg, Jones 2014, 72; Monaci 2017, 2856; Wiggins 2017, 26). Immersive experience directs the interpreters away from pondering about the reliability of the bits of information and activates the approximate and associative creation of connections that is, as we demonstrated in the subchapter "The model of meaning-making on the basis of the code text of conspiracy theories", extremely characteristic of semiosis that keeps discovering conspiracies.

In order to arouse interest in the audience, keep the enthusiasm for interpretation alive and trigger associative making of connections, specific multimodal text communities and semantic triggers inviting so-to-say active contributions to interpretation are often used. Before we move to particular examples, we shall concisely explain the nature of such triggers and their logic of functioning. To put it briefly, semantic triggers are textual constructions that guide the interpreters towards creating meaning relationships that are not explicitly presented in the text, that is, drawing conclusions, making comparisons and oppositions, generating hypotheses concerning the characters and the course of events, etc. Their task is to stir the desire for immersive experience in the Model Reader and, at the same time, to smother the processes of evaluating such relations critically and analytically (see Monaci 2017, 2842). Sara Monaci has pointed out that in strategic transmedia narratives, triggers can be "either symbolic items or explicit references [e.g. hyperlinks – *authors comment*, M.-L.M, A.V] to other media contents dispersed in the story world. They invite the user to explore all of the different available media, seeking further hints to better understand the topics" (2017, 2848). Monaci (2017, 2849) suggests that triggers guide the interpreter towards filling the semantic gaps in the storyworld through hints received with the help of intertextual references, which makes meaning transfer and the additive comprehension of the narrative possible. Perceiving the semantic gaps creates a necessary precondition for the functioning of meaning triggers, a situation of a certain meaning explosion in which unpredictability and ambiguity reign, which invites the interpreters to create order in the confusion of meanings on their own. Semantic triggers, governed by the strategic narrators, function as interpretative keys or anchors to which Model Readers can attach their interpretation paths. Effective anchors point at texts present in the memory of the interpretative community or that cause a strong affective reaction which will determine the further interpretation path or at least its tone. By using several reciprocally supportive triggers and systematically pointing at the relations contained in the memory of the interpretative community, it is possible to direct the Model Reader's interpretation process towards desired meanings (Monaci 2017, 2849).

In the subchapter "The model of meaning-making on the basis of the code text of conspiracy theories", we discussed more thoroughly the extremely adaptivist meaning-making based on the code text of conspiracy theories, which can bring together seemingly totally separate information fragments through the conspirators' ill will and misdeeds. It seems to us that transmedia narrating allows for a particularly powerful language of expression in the case of strategic conspiracy narratives as it makes it possible, due its immersive effect, to inform the audience in detail about the conspiracy scenario, as well as increase its meaningfulness and let even sceptical members of the interpretative community become used to such explanation schemes. The familiarity of the conspiracy theory is important, for constant repetition of such connections makes the code text more natural and allows it to accumulate additional meanings accompanying its manifestations in different contexts. Thus, it becomes ever more likely that the interpreter will use these connections spontaneously in future interpretative situations. We hold the opinion that transmedia campaigns can amplify semiosis based on the code text of conspiracy theories and direct the Model Reader towards ever new materials demonstrating the existence of the conspiracy. Stories of a secret villainous group that are strategically disseminated across several platforms can trigger an enthusiastic search for hidden clues and missing links from all possible sources, see e.g. the case of Pizzagate (see subchapter "The role of social media influencers in the shaping of conflict") and a cascade of sharing respective findings on social media.

Dominant textual strategies of transmedia storytelling

The following subchapter proceeds from the theories of cultural semiotics to explain the central meaning-making devices of strategic transmedia conspiracy narratives; we also illustrate these with some examples deriving from the Estonian right-wing populist information space. We focus on the EKRE web publication Uued Uudised and the web publication Objektiiv, an organ of the Foundation for the Protection of Family and Tradition (SAPTK), as these are the main Estonian-language channels in which transmedia storytelling is used to transmit Soros-themed conspiracy theories. These web publications are undoubtedly important nodes in the right-wing populist information field of Estonia. Due to sharing and copying of their content, readers of various forums, social media groups and blogs are familiar with the materials published there in addition to the right-wing base audience of these pages (see Kasekamp et al. 2019, 48). Also, the professional press often refers to stories published there. Both Uued Uudised as well as Objektiiv construct their narratives mediated by news and opinion pieces, radio programmes, video reportages and talk shows, and both channels amplify the contents on their official social media channels. The stories, told with the help of the different media, contain many repetitions of content and rhetoric and involve multiple cross-references with texts that have previously appeared on the same channel, as well as other publications that also support right-wing conservative ideology. Objektiiv and Uued Uudised also share each other's materials and their mutual cooperation has been underlined in an interview by Urmas Espenberg, the former executive publisher of Uued Uudised and member of the board of EKRE (see Saavik 2017, 25). Both channels have published dozens of stories on Soros's evil intentions and his hidden network of influence via textual, visual, acoustic as well as audio-visual media. Recurrent themes have been connecting Soros and his foundations with cultural Marxist brainwashing and the Central European immigration caravan (see subchapters: "Political conspiracy narrative: opposition to the elite" and "Conspiracy narrative of alternative knowledge: representing a decadent conspiracy system"); starting from autumn 2019, connections have been made with propaganda advocating counteracting climate change and organising fake protests.

In order to achieve narrative coherence, Uued Uudised and Objektiiv employ strategies described in several previous chapters. Presenting invariant connections of the Soros-themed conspiracy narrative (Soros as the main puppet master of the globalist network of evil and destroyer of nation states and traditional family and gender roles) through various columns and spokespersons can be identified as one of the basic devices used on these channels. Thus, connections of the strategic conspiracy narrative become fixed, yet at the same time the codes and points of view through which they are represented are varied. For instance, conspiracy narratives representing Soros as the scapegoat resurface at times in opinion pieces (Tõnisson 2018, 2019; Arro 2019), where they are represented as the result of the personal interpretation and analysis by a particular author, editorials in which they are presented as informed positions of the publication's editors (Eesti 200 … 2018; Jürgen Rooste … 2019; Trump tuleb … 2017) or EKRE and the Foundation for the Protection of Family and Tradition, and in the International column (Trumpi tagandamiskatse … 2019; Poola proovib … 2019; Skandaalne Soros … 2019) where they are presented as information from reputable sources (e.g. Breitbart, LifeSiteNews, InfoWars, Voice of Europe) on events occurring in the world.

Cohesion is created between different narrative entries also via consistent basic vocabulary and intertextual references. For instance, texts referring to Soros repeatedly employ phrases such as *globalism, Soros supporters, Soros Express, cultural Marxism, deep state, NWO, brainwashing, homosexual propaganda*. Such phrases contain strong hints at conspiracies and, as a rule, they are not used outside the extreme right-wing discourse. At the same time, the experienced members of the audiences of Objektiiv and Uued Uudised are quite likely to be familiar with these and are reminded of the general framework of relations of the conspiracy theory code text and concrete references at conspiracies made in this connection. Both Uued Uudised and Objektiiv use a system of keywords, categorising the articles, which also creates cohesion between different versions of the same narrative, while the interpreter can even reach entries from several years prior when clicking on promising keywords. The posts on the topic of Soros contain such recurrent keywords as *George Soros, immigration, Hungary, the Open Estonia Foundation* and *fake citizen society*. Ideological hypercoding is used consistently to position groups who hold views opposed to the nationalist conservative/extreme-right-wing world view as inherently dangerous; for this purpose, war rhetoric, the anti-Semitic tropes, as well as connecting opponents with sexual taboos and a generally lax morality, are used (see subchapter "Conspiracy narrative of alternative knowledge: representing a decadent conspiracy system").

In addition, the recurrent, and at times even periodic, appearance of EKRE and SAPTK spokespeople and their performances, provides repetition and creates cohesion. For instance, Uued Uudised shares a radio programme "Let's discuss the matter" ("Räägime asjast") by the EKRE leader Mart Helme and the leader of the party's Parliament faction Martin Helme, and often makes written summaries of the most important statements made in the programme. The programme has at times touched upon the Soros conspiracy ("Räägime asjast" ... 2019); still, it cannot be considered a recurring theme on the show. Nevertheless, conspiracy theories accusing the elite more generally frequently appear on the show and so it creates a favourable context for spreading conspiracy narratives with strategic aims. Almost every week, Objektiiv transmits a behind-the-desk talk show "In Focus" ("Fookuses") with the SAPTK board members, that primarily focuses on attacks against Christian moral norms and family values allegedly taking place in the Estonian context, as well as on the purportedly biased nature of the mainstream media and educational system (the general logic of conspiracy narratives with this thematic focus was explained in the subchapter "Conspiracy narrative of alternative knowledge: representing a decadent conspiracy system"). From the point of view of creating narrative cohesion it is also remarkable for the show repeats and amplifies the main story points of the articles that have appeared on Objektiiv.

The creators of strategic narratives quite often employ (audio-)visual representations as interpreters process them quickly and visuals have a strong affective effect. The scholar of visual rhetoric Anthony Blair (2004, 51) has underscored that, differently from processing various verbal (particularly written) messages, we are able to receive visual information effortlessly for a short time and that visuals have a specific ability "to convey a narrative in a short time". The reception of visual texts is made specific also by the fact that their processing does not so much depend on the will and deliberate choices of the interpreter, but that they wield unmediated influence and call forth partly subconscious reactions in many ways (Blair 2004, 51). A stimulus with an affective load is more relevant for the interpreter and is processed more quickly and more intensive attention is focused on it (von Stackelberg, Jones 2014, 63; see Sunstein, Vermeule 2009, 216). It is because of this quality that visuals function as effective keys or anchors of interpretation; they allow activation of a certain predisposition and memory connections before experiencing other narrative layers, which will direct the ensuing text processing to a major extent. This will guide the Model Reader towards an intuitive attribution of a unified meaning of the fragments of information received, as well as the narrative uniting of these into a mental whole (Ventsel, Madisson 2017), which can be expressed, for instance, in a snap judgement of the development as benevolent or destruction- and chaos-related, and judging the relevant actors as agents of Good or Evil.

As a rule, Soros-themed conspiracy narratives are illustrated with four types of visuals. Quite often, Soros's portrait photos are used (George Soros ... 2019; Poola proovib ... 2019; Skandaalne Soros ... 2019), that focus on the billionaire's face and usually represent him in a public speaking situation with microphones turned towards him, while the logo of an influential international organisation, e.g. the European Union, can be seen in the background. Such visuals trigger associations that support the image of Soros as an influential agent who forcefully spreads his messages in corridors of power, and also contributes to the identification of an omnipotent conspiracy system with Soros's person.

Visuals of the second type represent the masses of people whom Soros's instigations are reported to have set on the move. For instance, photos and videos of protest marches for women's or LGBT rights, or gatherings in the name of media and citizen freedoms are fairly widespread (President Donald ... 2018; Vaher 2019; Ungari valitsus ... 2018), as are images of people who have arrived in Europe or North America due to the migration crisis (Kui Trump ... 2018; Rändekriis vahemerel ... 2018; Ühe majanduspõgenikust ... 2018). Images and videos of protests focus on active and mobile masses of people who proclaim their message with shouting and slogans. Migrants who have arrived via the so-called *Soros Express* are usually shown in a passive position, e.g. sitting. In both cases it is not particular individuals who are foregrounded, but rather an impression of a homogenous mass of people. Neither are there concrete references to Soros or organisations financed by him; such connections are created only in the texts that are positioned next to the visuals. Thus, an interpreter who is oriented at an immersive story experience has to generate the respective juxtaposition between the images of masses of people and Soros's manipulations when interpreting particular visuals. When the Model Reader is actively actualised in the interpreter, the added pictorial material will seem as convincing evidence of the topicality of the conspiracy. Together with the textual component, the pictorial materials referred to amplify a single main message connected with Soros – that he and other top globalists share an ability to subtly manipulate various groups and stir them to concrete actions, while particular groups (feminists, human rights activists, migrants, etc.), and individuals constituting these, are not represented as independent active agents, but rather as the conspirators' puppets (see the subchapter "Conspiracy narrative of alternative knowledge: representing a decadent conspiracy system"). In connection with protest marches, the means of influencing on the part of Soros get highlighted, such as cultural Marxist/liberal leftish brainwashing and sums reportedly paid to the protesters for taking to the streets. Migrants are represented as particularly passive agents who blindly follow the call of Soros to come to Europe and North America in search of a better life, and are turned into a dangerous means in the grand plan of undermining nation states without being aware of this themselves.

The third type of visuals represent the Fidesz posters that appeared in the streets of Hungary in connection with the general elections of 2018. On the left-hand side of the poster, there is a smiling portrait of Soros in black and white; the right-hand side depicts the Hungarian flag, a Hungarian-language reference in a small font to a poll conducted in 2017 that claimed that 99 per cent of Hungarians were against illegal immigration, and under this in block capitals "Ne hagyjuk hogy Soros nevessen a végén" [*Don't let Soros have the last laugh*]. It is remarkable that both Objektiiv and Uued Uudised have been repeatedly sharing pictures of this poster for three whole years, not only a digital version, but also photos of them in Hungarian public spaces; e.g. they can be recognised as being located in the underground (Valitsus: Ungari ... 2018), close to parking lots (Ungaris toimub ... 2017) or on bus stops (Rahvusriike vaenav ... 2018), etc. Objektiiv has also added captions contextualising the posters, e.g. "An escalator in the Budapest Underground carrying Hungarians past posters ordered by the Government that are warning them against Soros's machinations" and "Hungarian Government's poster warning against the activities of George Soros". Such visuals help to amplify the message presented in the text that the ruling powers in Hungary are taking Soros's machinations, as well as the dangers proceeding from these, seriously and citizens should not allow the elderly billionaire to enforce his manipulations as easily as he has reportedly been able to previously. Such pictures confirm the image of Soros as a dangerous adversary, and they also trigger a positive recognition in the Model Reader that EKRE and SAPTK have strong Hungarian allies in their fight against *Soros supporters, globalists* and *leftist extremists*.

The fourth type of visual is an image with a large stylised picture of Soros in the foreground, while the background represents slogans against misogyny, rainbow flags and people wearing the pink hats known from the Women's March in 2017. The visual is telling for several reasons: first, it has the status of a certain iconic image in the context of Uued Uudised as it has repeatedly been published with texts discussing Soros's various secret plans (Sorose rahastavad ... 2018; Rahvusriikide lammutaja ... 2019; Ungari annab ... 2018) (also the picture of the poster described in the previous paragraph and some images depicting Soros in conference situations have been employed repeatedly). Second, the stylised quality of the image of Soros and its strong symbolic charge can be noticed against the visual background of Uued Uudised that, as a rule, represents photographic realism. In comparison with the protesters, the Soros figure in a black hooded cape appears to be large than life, towering over the masses, and his forceful stare is directed at the viewer. Soros's clothing recalls the ritual robe known from popular culture that is fairly widespread in the visual representations of the Illuminati. Such clothes are also used to depict the Grim Reaper or Palpatine – a fictional character in the Star Wars. The association with a dark, or even deadly, force is amplified by the black fingernails of Soros's outstretched hand, which appear as if they had been scraping the earth. The texts represented together with these visuals speak of the "Stop Soros" package of Hungarian bills; concrete planned punishment measures that are claimed to be into use against Soros's alleged minions, and the danger of the possibility that the "globalism and multiculturalism propaganda" promoted by Soros might influence the results of the 2019 parliamentary elections. Thus, none of these texts have any other direct links to the visuals besides the fact that both represent Soros. Again, it is a situation that requires active interpretative contribution from a Model Reader interested in a nuanced experience of the storyworld. Such an image will call forth a stronger affective resonance than the visuals described above and grip the interpreter's attention. It is likely to provoke a feeling of unease in the Model Reader and function as a semantic trigger that unleashes associations between Soros and non-human powers of Evil. It will help to corroborate the non-discrete core of meaning of the conspiracy theory's code text, which, in brief, consists of recognising that the conspirators deliberately engage in evil-doing and cause suffering to large numbers of people as they are inherently Evil, and thus all persons and enterprises even remotely connected to them deserve unambiguous condemnation due to their contact with such Evil.

Functions of transmedia storytelling

It has been noticed that non-functional transmedia narratives that are perceived by their addressees as first and foremost representations pointing at, as it were, real actors, settings and events, have a stronger potential to mobilise the audience to particular action and trigger active content-making than fictional stories (Freeman 2016, 95). The function of transmedia storytelling is creating narrative cohesion on the textual level, on the one hand, as well as fixing it in the memory of interpretative community by repeating it in different sign systems. On the other hand, its aim is to guide the interpretation paths of the targeted audience. The Model Reader is awakened with various strategic textual devices – semantic gaps, visual texts triggering affective semiosis, etc. The Model Reader should actualise the interpretation paths supporting the strategic aims and make his or her contribution based on interpretative collaboration, to legitimising a particular political agenda or undermining the adversaries' world view.

As under strategic narrative we mean targeted communication, it may seem slightly paradoxical that it should be textual elements that cause a certain discord, ambivalence or inaccuracies, or semantic gaps, that call forth interpretative activity on part of the reader. We find that based on the conception of Lotman's effect of the trope it is possible to explicate the meaning-making logic and demonstrate its functioning principles in the context of transmedial storytelling of the conspiracy narrative. In summary, Lotman treats the effect of the trope as a powerful mechanism of creating new meanings that is triggered when, in a certain interpretative context, a relationship of correspondence is generated between two elements that have mutually incompatible meanings or, in terms of cultural semiotics, are discretely and non-discretely encoded (Lotman 2000, 37; see also the subchapter "Discrete and non-discrete logic of code-textual meaning-making").

In the context of strategic conspiracy narratives, we can give the description of temporal and logical-causal circumstances as examples of discrete elements, and the outlining of the inhuman malevolence and horror of the suffering caused by them as non-discrete ones (this can be done particularly effectively via videos and pictures). A universal characteristic of the trope is that one of the elements will always remain discrete and the other non-discrete, while the chasm of their mutual untranslatability based on principle will cause the need in the interpreter to find an explanation level relating them to each other (Lotman 2000, 37–38). The search for an explanation level fascinates the interpreter who cannot be content with the flourishing of ambivalence and equivocation, a creative process of generating correspondences is activated in him or her due to the desire for narrative sense-making. Historical narration related to daily life is mostly based on discrete creation of links; what is mediated is events that are connected into a temporal-causal sequence, but when this is enriched by non-discrete elements through the effect of the trope, a certain tendency of generating patterns and unified meanings is added (Lotman 2006, 283). In the case of conspiracy narratives, such unified meaning is expressed in the recognition that many events perceived as unpleasant, as well as broader social processes, are part of something larger than a mere sequence of unpleasant developments; that this is a continuous manifestation of the same Evil. Thus, visuals and semantic gaps make it possible to turn discrete events connected with conspiracies affectively more attractive; they often provide an important impulse for locating concrete circumstances and actors on the axis of good–evil/morality–decadence as universal unified meaning. Also, it is possible to create relationships of correspondence between contemporary events and a mythical past via strategically constructed semantic gaps and triggers, and blend heroism and emotional tension into the representation of the conflict between the own and the alien by using powerful visuals and a dramatic sound language.

Notes

1 *Crossmedia* and *transmedia* are often used as parallel concepts in academic discourse (Saldre, Torop 2012, 25); the former is mostly associated with studies of the marketing and entertainment industry, while the latter more frequently appears in studies of artistic texts and the adaptation of concrete textual motifs. Semioticians of culture Maarja Ojamaa and Peeter Torop emphasise that *crossmedia* allows them to establish a narrower focus on studying receiver-centred and intentional communication strategies, while the concept of *transmedia* makes it possible to treat the audience's content creation and broader processes of cultural signification, including those connected with cultural memory and dynamics of culture (Ojamaa 2015, 9; Ojamaa, Torop 2015, 11). In our book we are using the term *transmedia* throughout as it has been widely employed in studies dedicated to strategic narratives and as we are interested in both strategic communication of the code text of conspiracy theory on different platforms and their spontaneous emergence in the audience's interpretative activities and content creation.
2 An image becomes iconic if it frequently appears across media channels and audiences associate it with a certain news event (Perlmutter 1998).

5   Conclusion and future directions

In the past decade, various online platforms, especially social media, have developed into a central information and communication space in which the collective meaning of conflicts is strategically constructed, and people's decision-making processes are influenced. Thus, in the context of the techniques of informational influencing activities, analysis of the so-called soft manifestations of power that are discursive and take into consideration the special characteristics of social media have become ever more important: how to attract attention? How to shape narratives that would address the audience on the background of a general abundance of information? How to construct texts so that the targeted audience will share them and thus contribute to the dissemination of strategic narratives?

Attribution, or challenges that are connected with detecting the author or formulator of a particular narrative, has been pointed out as one of the significant research problems in analysing strategic narratives circulating on the Internet. The subchapter "Information conflicts and information warfare" identified that the contemporary information war which embraces hybrid media spheres, has led to important shifts in the meaning of war, as differentiation between actions coordinated by state/non-state institutions and those belonging to the civil sphere of ordinary citizens is ever more difficult. Our study did not focus on the attribution of the primary authorship of the narrative or the detection of the central instance coordinating its dissemination, but we directed our main attention at textual strategies through which the audience's interpretation paths are being guided on the discursive level. This approach proceeds from the premise that we can speak of a strategic narrative when it is possible to detect an aim presented in it. The unified aim can become manifested both in narratives disseminated by state as well as non-state actors; thus we made no clear differentiation between the level of the strategic author or the formation level, and the level of dissemination of narratives or the projection level.

In this book we mostly proceeded from the treatment of the strategic narrative, and the theory and method of cultural semiotics. The book's central focus of analysis is the discursive shaping of a conflict between the own and the alien in strategic narratives. We conceptualised the conflict as a gap between different systems of meaning constructed and mediated in informational influencing activities via different semiotic means. In Part II we analysed conspiracy narratives that represented the world-famous figure of George Soros as the main puppet master of any number of conspiracies. On the level of discourse, the Soros-themed conspiracy narrative functions as a code text that helps to embrace social groups that at first glance seem to be totally separate, yet are represented either as the billionaire's minions or victims of the conspiracy organised by him. In order to guide the audience's interpretation process, the Model Reader, or the ideal receiver, as it were, is shaped in the narratives by the author or disseminator of strategic narratives. The role of Model Reader is to actualises the codes and intertextual references that have been strategically planned into narratives in order to guide the audience's interpretation process. In the examples we have analysed, the Model Reader's interpretation paths were most clearly guided by the topic – the conflict – between Soros and those suffering due to his actions. Its antithetical-antagonistic or agonistic character in many ways determined the textual strategies employed in constructing the conspiracy narrative.

In the analysis section of the book, we exemplified the textual strategies through which it is possible to construct narrative unity. One of the main textual strategic devices in the conspiracy narratives connected with Soros is the war scenario. It first and foremost characterises our political narratives, but also alternative knowledge ones in which *our* value world is constructed via an antithetical opposition to the value worlds of the *conspirators*. Political narratives are often constructed as endangering *our* existence. Often they are based on the textual strategy of creating analogies with historical events, for instance, it is indicated that Soros's activities display the same signs that can be detected in the unleashing of wars that have taken place recently. Conspiracy narratives of alternative knowledge, however, present the financier as an instigator of processes of a long duration that have led to moral decline. Marketing conspiracy narratives are based on a more ambivalent and playful conflict in which the opposing force is represented as an omnipotent, yet at the same time glamorous, villain. The aim of marketing the cultivation of conspiracy associations is primarily to catch the audience's attention and keep it on the meaning world linked with their brand for as long as possible through mysteriousness and the effect of infotainment.

The fourth chapter explained the role of affective semiosis and transmedial narrating in amplifying the potential of strategic narratives for attention grabbing and viral spread. We showed which discursive means (e.g. signs connected with fear) can trigger affective semiosis that serves as an important precondition for the emergence of connective-action-based audiences. As regards strategic transmedia storytelling, we highlighted devices that help make the storyworld more nuanced both on emotional as well as informational planes, and also those devices that create cohesion between different fragments of the story.

Due to the setup of the problem, the framework we are offering will cover only a single stretch in studying strategic communication that involves several parties and versatile dissemination channels. The scope of the book does not allow the conducting of a deep analysis of different aspects of complex trans-platform storytelling; rather, we concentrate on some representative examples that reveal the potential of transmedia storytelling and illustrate the basic textual strategies. Neither did we treat in detail the sign-typological basic mechanism of affective meaning-making that causes intense reactions in the interpreter. In this book we have only pointed at the discourse of fear and happiness as a necessary context, and signs expressing this that trigger specific semiosis in the audience. In the following, we will give a brief outline of how future studies could contribute to the applicability of the semiotic theory presented in this book in more comprehensive analyses of strategic social media communication.

Sketching the methodology of social media strategic conspiracy narratives

One of the most important steps in the further development of our approach would be a thorough application of our theoretical framework in analysing an empirical text corpus. The main challenge concerning this is the delimiting and categorisation of the material to be analysed under the conditions of the informational superabundance on social media. Another difficulty that arises in connection with the text corpus studied is that we must take into account that social-media-dominated public communication is marked by proliferation of (audio-)visual and viral content. Such text creation is based on "the interconnection of texts and images" where "the text is often an integral part of the image and the same applies vice versa" (Kovács 2015, 67). Different visually oriented texts enable the reinforcing of messages through an emotional impact, which makes the ideas graspable for a potentially very wide audience (Monaci 2017, 2852; Leone 2019), and often such discourses are driven by affective meaning-making (Prøitz 2017). In our estimation it seems promising to proceed from Peirce's triadic division of types of sign – icons, indexes and symbols – and analyse in more depth which intensity each type of sign evokes in the triggering of affective semiosis, whether, and how, affective semiosis is influenced by the coeffect of multimodal texts, etc.

Taking into account the significance of visual meaning-making we need to combine the multimodal approach (Kress 2012; O'Halloran et al. 2013) with using various data collecting programs. It seems to us that the use of programs such as Multimodal Analysis Image (http://multimodal-analysis.com/products/multimodal-analysis-image) could prove effective, as it can be used to collect and analyse data (hashtags, visual viral texts/symbols, etc.) in the first phases of semiotic content analysis, which is helpful in preparing material for analysis. Kay O'Halloran et al., who developed the method of semiotic multimodal discourse analysis, points out that "this approach is motivated by the idea that if two annotation units are 'not related' in time, then it does not make sense to consider these units in the pattern" (2013, 674). This means that such a passage will make it possible to detect certain patterns occurring in the preliminary data, as regards different key words, dominant signifiers and images. "Further filtering of pattern histogram (accurate representation of the distribution of data – *authors' comment* M-L.M, A.V) can be done based on the assumption that one may be interested in more repeated patterns than in less repeated ones. This approach favours highly repeated patterns over less frequent patterns and greatly reduces the total number of patterns in the histogram, making it easier to interpret manually" (ibid.). It was pointed out in the chapter on transmedia storytelling that the repetition of certain textual elements creates cohesion on the level of the text and contributes to it becoming fixed in the audience's memory. Repetition can be regarded as a special characteristic of the strategic narrative (Zhabotynska, Velivchenko 2019, 361). Thus, the quantitative level of collecting data can help to detect the most relevant and representative texts for qualitative analysis that is conducted manually and so proves to be resource intensive.

The first stage of the research – categorising the data based on the patterns – would be followed by the second stage of classification. Proceeding from the research questions posed, the data, that have been provisionally mapped and categorised, can be classified under broader categories: key topics, attributions of agency and visual representations of *us* and *the other*. This categorisation will help to reveal how conflicts are presented from different cultural-political perspectives and platforms and how these issues are constructing networked publics. At this stage it is possible to employ the model presented in this book that allows for detecting text-strategic devices for constructing the Model Reader and the Model Author, as well as aims set by the strategic narrative.

The qualitative approach also means an abductive move in the methodology: semiotic analysis of patterns that have already been detected can give results in which it is possible to detect different strategic aims behind larger clusters of repetitive patterns. This is apparent, for instance, in situations in which appropriation of the strategic narrative occurs, that is, keywords that seem similar are used to achieve opposite aims. However, this can be detected primarily with the help of qualitative studies. Here, scholars again meet the question of attribution mentioned above, but answering it presumes different methods of analysis than those offered by text-level analysis of strategic narratives. This should involve a complex study of other policies, e.g. of how some narratives overlap with other actions of certain (state or non-state) actors both on the home scene and abroad (for more, see Roselle et al. 2014; O'Loughlin et al. 2017). However, applying the model we have offered will help those conducting such a complex study ask relevant research questions and set up hypotheses.

The research direction described above could primarily focus on the level of the formation and projection of strategic narratives. To study the reception level, the analysis of interpretive experiences of individuals visiting conspiracy sites should be focused on, while enquiring if different types of users emerge there and asking which factors facilitate active content creation on the part of the audience. This direction could be complemented by multi-site digital ethnography (Hine 2015), while conducting projective group interviews makes it possible to analyse how the participants in online communication themselves describe the role of narratives.

What is the use of studying strategic conspiracy narratives?

The question posed in this title is our final one; it closes the book and, rather, serves as a rhetorical one. Our concentrating on the analysis of conspiracy narratives in this study does not mean that the semiotic approach we have developed would have no explanatory power in the context of other strategic narratives. Due to their code-textual centre, strategic conspiracy narratives emerge as stories with a fixed structure and great explanatory force, but similar textual strategies can also be identified in narratives that do not presume the existence of a malevolent group of a criminal inclination. Thus, the framework we have proposed can be used to analyse the textual strategies of any strategic narrative.

Taking the above into consideration, it can be claimed that this book contributes to a more general understanding of problems connected with information security. Lately, democratic countries have increasingly been compelled to counter such problems manifesting as, for instance, fake news or proliferation of manipulative texts. The analysis of different semiotic strategies of modelling the opponent – antithesis and agonism – will also be useful in understanding the context that connects conspiracy-theoretical thought with populism and radicalisation. Humans are not born with radical or populist views, neither are they conspiracy theorists from the beginning. In addition to economic (economic inequality between people, differences in the accessibility of social services, etc.) and social conditions (the society's level of education, gender and age ratio, etc.), also systems of meaning in which we live and which shape our understanding of the world have their role in a person's radicalisation or adopting beliefs regarding conspiracies. Disciplines of both humanities and social sciences can contribute to the study of this circle of problems. This book proposes a novel semiotic perspective for analysing contemporary strategic communication.

Bibliography

Abidin, Crystal 2018. *Internet Celebrity: Understanding Fame Online*. Bingley: Emerald Publishing.

Ahmed, Sara 2010. *The Promise of Happiness*. Durham: Duke University.

Alexievich, Svetlana 2016. *Secondhand Time: The Last of the Soviets*. New York: Random House.

Altheide, David 2002. *Creating Fear: News and the Construction of Crisis*. Hawthorne, New York: de Gruyter.

American Antichrist and Soros are Spreading Chaos in Post-Soviet Space 2019. *EU versus Disinformation* 21.06. https://euvsdisinfo.eu/report/american-antichrist-and-soros-are-spreading-chaos-in-post-soviet-space/.

Andrejevic, Mark 2013. *Infoglut: How too Much Information is Changing the Way we Think and Know*. New York: Routledge.

Antoniades, Andreas; O'Loughlin, Ben; Miskimmon, Alister 2010. Great power politics and strategic narratives. *Working paper no. 7*. The Centre for Global Political Economy, University of Sussex.

Armstrong, Sean 2009. Stalin's Witch-hunt: Magical Thinking in the Great Terror. *Totalitarian Movements and Political Religions*, 3, 221–240.

Arro, Kaspar 2019. Milline Euroopa meil meeles mõlgub? *Uued Uudised* 18.05. https://uueduudised.ee/arvamus/kaspar-arro-milline-euroopa-meil-meeles-molgub/.

Askanius, Tina; Mylonas, Yiannis 2015. Extreme-right Responses to the European Economic Crisis in Denmark and Sweden: The Discursive Construction of Scapegoats and Lodestars. *Javnost: The Public*, 22 (1), 55–72.

Astapova, Anastasiya 2017. In Search for Truth: Surveillance Rumors and Vernacular Panopticon in Belarus. *Journal of American Folklore*, 130 (517), 276–304.

Atton, Cris 2006. Far-right Media on the Internet: Culture, Discourse and Power. *New Media & Society*, 8, 573–587.

Aupers, Stef 2012. "Trust No One": Modernization, Paranoia and Conspiracy Culture. *European Journal of Communication*, 27 (1), 22–34.

Ballinger, Dean 2011. *Conspiratoria: The Internet and the Logic of Conspiracy Theory*. The University of Waikato, the department of Screen and Media Studies. Doctoral thesis.

Barkun, Michael 2003. *A Culture of Conspiracy: Apocalyptic Visions in Contemporary America*. Los Angeles: University of California Press.

Barthes, Roland 1980. From Work to Text. In: *Image-Music-text*, (trans. S. Heath). New York: Hill and Wang, 155–164.

Benkler, Yochai; Faris, Robert; Roberts, Hal 2018. *Network Propaganda: Manipulation, Disinformation, and Radicalization in American Politics*. New York: Oxford University Press.

Bennett, Lance; Segerberg, Alexandra 2012. The Logic of Connective Action. *Information, Communication and Society*, 15 (5), 739–768.

Berger, John M. 2016. *Nazis vs. ISIS on Twitter: A Comparative Study of White Nationalist and ISIS Online Social Media Networks*. Washington: George Washington University Program on Extremism Report.

Bergmann, Eirikur 2018. *Conspiracy & Populism the Politics of Misinformation*. Cham: Palgrave Macmillan.

Bessi, Alessandro; Coletto, Mauro; Davidescu, George Alexandru; Scala, Antonio; Caldarelli, Guido; Quattrociocchi, Walter 2015a. Science vs Conspiracy: Collective Narratives in the Age of Misinformation. *PLOS ONE*, 10 (2), 1–17.

Bessi, Alessandro; Zollo, Fabiana; Del Vicario, Michela; Puliga, Michelangelo; Scala, Antonio; Caldarelli, Guido; Uzzi, Brian; Quattrociocchi, Walter 2016. Users Polarization on Facebook and YouTube. *PLOS ONE*, 11 (8), 1–24.

Bessi, Alessandro; Zollo, Fabiana; Del Vicario, Michela; Scala, Antonio; Caldarelli, Guido; Quattrociocchi, Walter 2015b. Trend of Narratives in the Age of Misinformation. *PLOS ONE*, 10 (8), 1–16.

Birchall, Clare 2006. *Knowledge Goes Pop*. Oxford, New York: Berg.

Blair, Anthony J. 2004. The Rhetoric of Visual Arguments. In: *Defining Visual Rhetoric*, (eds. C. Hill; M. Helmers). New Jersey: LEA, 41–62.

Bockstette, Carsten 2008. *Jihadist Terrorist Use of Strategic Communication Management Techniques. The Marshall Center Occasional Paper Series*. The George C. Marshall European Center for Security Studies.

Bondarenko, Veronika 2017. George Soros is a Favorite Target of the Right — Here's How That Happened. *Business Insider* 20.05, www.businessinsider.com/how-did-george-soros-become-the-favorite-boogeyman-of-the-right-2017-5?r=UK.

Boros, Tamás 2018. The Hungarian "STOP Soros" Act: Why Does the Government Fight Human Rights Organisations? https://library.fes.de/pdf-files/bueros/budapest/14205.pdf.

Boym, Svetlana 1999. Conspiracy Theories and Literary Ethics: Umberto Eco, Danilo Kiš and The Protocols of Zion. *Comparative Literature*, 51 (2), 97–122.

Branco, Angela; Valsiner, Jaan 2010. Towards Cultural Psychology of Affective Processes: Semiotic Regulation of Dynamic Fields. *Estudios de Psicología*, 31 (3), 243–251.

Bratich, Jack Z. 2004. Trust No One (on the Internet): The CIA-Crack-Contra Conspiracy Theory and Professional Journalism. *TELEVISION & NEW MEDIA*, 5 (2), 109–139.

Bratich, Jack Z. 2008. *Conspiracy Panics: Political Rationality and Popular Culture*. Albany: State University of New York Press.

Brazzoli, Mario S. 2007. Future Prospects of Information Warfare and Particularly Psychological Operations. In: *South African Army Vision 2020*, (ed. L. le Roux). Pretoria: Institute for Security Studies, 217–232.

Broniatowski, David A.; Jamison, Amelia M.; Qi, SiHua; Al Kulaib, Lulwah; Chen, Tao; Benton, Adrian; Quinn, Sandra; Dredze, Mark 2018. PhD Weaponized Health Communication: Twitter Bots and Russian Trolls Amplify the Vaccine Debate. *AJPH OPEN-THEMED RESEARCH*, 108 (10), 1378–1384.

Buchbender, Ortwin 1989. Zentrum des Bosen. Zur Genesis National-sozialistischer Feinbilder. In: *Feinbild. Geschichte – Dokumentation – Problematik*, (ed. G. Wagenlehner). Frankfurt am Main: Report Verlag, 17–57.

Butter, Michael 2014. *Plots, Designs, and Schemes: American Conspiracy Theories from the Puritans to the Present.* Berlin/Boston: de Gruyter.

Butter, Michael; Knight, Peter 2016. Bridging the Great Divide: Conspiracy Theory Research for the 21st Century. *DIOGENES,* 1–13.

Campbell, Alexandra 2008. Without "you" I'm Nothing: Making White Britishness Online. *Social Semiotics,* 18 (4), 409–424.

Campion-Vincent, Vèronique 2005. From Evil Others to Evil Elites: A Dominant Pattern in Conspiracy Theories Today. In: *Rumor Mills: The Social Impact of Rumor and Legend,* (eds. G.A. Fine; V. Campion-Vincent; C. Heath). New Jersey, New Brunswick: Transaction Publishers, 103–122.

Campion-Vincent, Vèronique 2015. Note sur les Entrepreneurs en Complots. *Dioge`ne,* 249–250, 99–106.

Caumanns, Ute; Önnerfson, Andreas 2020. Conspiracy Theories and Visual Culture. In: *Routledge Handbook of Conspiracy Theories 1st Edition,* (eds. M. Butter; P. Knight). New York: Routledge, 441–455.

Chadwick, Andrew 2009. Web 2.0: New Challenges for the Study of e-democracy in an Era of Informational Exuberance. *Journal of Law and Policy for the Information Society,* 5 (1), 10–42.

Cichocka, Aleksandra 2016. Understanding Defensive and Secure In-group Positivity: The Role of Collective Narcissism. *European Review of Social Psychology,* 27, 283–317.

Colăcel, Onoriu; Pintilescu, Corneliu 2017. From Literary Culture to Post-communist Media: Romanian Conspiracism. *Messages, Sages and Ages,* 4 (2), 31–40.

Conspiracy Theories about Billionaire George Soros Take Centre-stage in Hungarian Election 2018. *South China Morning Post* 18.03. www.scmp.com/news/world/europe/article/2137696/conspiracy-theories-about-billionaire-george-soros-take-centre.

Cronin, Blaise; Crawford, Holly 1999. Information Warfare: Its Application in Military and Civilian Contexts. *Information Society,* 15 (4), 257–263.

CrossTalk Bullhorns: Crazy World 2019. *Russia Today* 13.05. www.rt.com/shows/crosstalk/459178-trump-russia-foreign-policy/.

Dahlberg, Lincoln 2011. Re-constructing Digital Democracy: An Outline of Four "Positions". *New Media & Society,* 13 (6), 855–872.

Dahlgren, Peter 2006. Doing Citizenship: The Cultural Origins of Civic Agency in the Public Sphere. *European Journal of Cultural Studies,* 9 (3), 267–286.

Darczewska, Jolanta; Żochowski, Piotr 2015. Russophobia in the Kremlin's Strategy. A Weapon of Mass Destruction. *Point of View,* 56. Warsaw: Centre of East European Studies.

Davosis netihiiglaste hukku kuulutanud Soros pelgab tegelikult nende kontrollimatust 2018. *Uued Uudised* 28.01. https://uueduudised.ee/uudis/maailm/davosis-netihiiglaste-hukku-kuulutanud-soros-pelgab-tegelikult-nende-kontrollimatust/.

Dean, Jodi 2002. *Publicity's Secret: How Technoculture Capitalizes on Democracy.* Ithaca: Cornell University Press.

Dean, Jodi 2010. Affective Networks. *Media Tropes,* 2 (2), 19–44.

Del Vicario, Michela; Bessi, Alessandro; Zollo, Fabiana; Petroni, Fabio; Scala, Antonio; Caldarelli, Guido; Stanley, H. Eugene; Quattrociocchi, Walter 2016. The Spreading of Misinformation Online. *Proceedings of the National Academy of Sciences of the United States of America,* 113 (3), 554–559.

Denning, Dorothy E. 1999. *Information Warfare and Security.* Boston, MA: Addison-Wesley.

Dimitriu, George; De Graaf, Beatrice 2016. Fighting the War at Home: Strategic Narratives, Elite Responsiveness, and the Dutch Mission in Afghanistan, 2006–2010. *Foreign Policy Analysis*, 12 (1), 2–23.

Dispute Between Protesters and Police. There is a Rally Near Soros Office 2019. *Armenia Sputnik* 03.06. https://armeniasputnik.am/armenia/20190603/18946725/qashqshuk-akciayi-masnakicneri-u-vostikanutyan-mijev-sorosi-gtrasenyaki-mot-hanrahavaqe.html.

Donovan, Barna 2011. *Conspiracy Films: A Tour of Dark Places in the American Conscious*. Jefferson: McFarland & Company.

Eco, Umberto 1976. *A Theory of Semiotics*. London: Indiana University press.

Eco, Umberto 1990. *Interpretation and Overinterpretation*. Cambridge: World, History, Texts Tanner Lectures.

Eco, Umberto 2005. *Lector in fabula*. Tartu: Tartu University Press.

Eesti 200 – seda Soros rahastaks 2018. *Objektiiv* 23.08. https://objektiiv.ee/juhtkiri-eesti-200-seda-soros-rahastaks/.

Einstein, Katherine L.; Glick, David M. 2015. Do I Think BLS Data are BS? The Consequences of Conspiracy Theories. *Political Behavior*, 37 (3), 679–701.

Ekman, Mattias 2016. Online Islamophobia and the Politics of Fear: Manufacturing the Green Scare. *Ethnic and Racial Studies*, 38 (11), 1986–2002.

Evans, Elizabeth 2011. *Transmedia Television: Audiences, New Media, and Daily Life*. New York: Routledge.

Farkas, Johan; Schou, Jannick 2018. Fake News as a Floating Signifier: Hegemony, Antagonism and the Politics of Falsehood. *Javnost: The Public*, 25 (3), 298–314.

Fekete, Liz 2012. *Pedlars of Hate: The Violent Impact of the European Far Right*. London: Institute of Race Relations.

Feklyunina, Valentina 2013. Constructing Russophobia. In: *Russia's Identity in International Relations: Images, Perceptions, Misperceptions*, (ed. R. Taras). Routledge: London, 91–109.

Fenster, Mark 2008. *Conspiracy Theories: Secrecy and Power in American Culture*. Minneapolis, London: University of Minnesota Press.

Fiske, John 1994. *Media Matters: Everyday Culture and Political Change*. Minneapolis: University of Minnesota Press.

Flaherty, Emma; Roselle, Laura 2018. Contentious Narratives and Europe. Conspiracy Theories and Strategic Narratives Surrounding RT's Brexit News Coverage. *Journal of International Affairs*, 71, 53–60.

Foucault, Michel 1977. *Orders of Discourse*, (trans. R. Sawyer), *Social Science Information*, 10/2.

Foucault, Michel 1980. *Power/Knowledge: Selected Interviews and Other Writings 1972–1977*. New York: Pantheon Books.

Freedman, Lawrence 2006. Networks, Culture and Narratives. *The Adelphi Papers*, 45 (379), 11–26.

Freeman, Matthew 2016. Small Change–Big Difference: Tracking the Transmediality of Red Nose Day. *Journal of European Television History and Culture*, 5 (10), 87–96.

Frenkel, Sheera; Confessore, Nicholas; Kang, Cecilia; Rosenberg, Matthew; Nicas, Jack 2018. Delay, Deny and Deflect: How Facebook's Leaders Fought Through Crisis. *The New York Times*, www.nytimes.com/2018/11/14/technology/facebook-data-russia-election-racism.html.

Furedi, Frank 2019. *Kuidas hirm toimib. Hirmukultuur 21 sajandil*. Tallinn: Postimees.

Gaines-Ross, Leslie 2010. Reputation Warfare. *Harvard Business Review*, https://hbr.org/2010/12/reputation-warfare.

George Soros asutas USA valimiste mõjutamiseks super–sihtfondi 2019. *Objektiiv* 02.08. https://objektiiv.ee/george-soros-asutas-usa-valimiste-mojutamiseks-super-sihtfondi/.

George Soros – Euroopa vaenlane 2016. *Uued Uudised* 14.04. https://uueduudised.ee/uudis/maailm/george-soros-euroopa-vaenlane/.

Gergely, Andras 2015. Orban Accuses Soros of Stoking Refugee Wave to Weaken Europe. *Bloomberg* 30.10. www.bloomberg.com/news/articles/2015-10-30/orban-accuses-soros-of-stoking-refugee-wave-to-weaken-europe.

Giry, Julien 2015. Le movement LaRouche a` l'international. Impact du territoire et stratégies politiques d'implantation a` l'échelle nationale et locale. Approche comparée France/Etats-Unis. *Politeïa*, 28, 433–452.

Giry, Julien; Gürpınar, Doğan 2020. Functions and Uses of Conspiracy Theories in Authoritarian Regimes. In: *Routledge Handbook of Conspiracy Theories 1st Edition*, (eds. M. Butter, P. Knight). New York: Routledge, 317–328.

Golec de Zavala, Agnieszka; Cichocka, Aleksandra; Eidelson, Roy; Jayawickreme, Nuwan 2009. Collective Narcissism and its Social Consequences. *Journal of Personality and Social Psychology*, 97, 1074–1096.

Golec de Zavala, Agnieszka; Peker, Müjde; Guerra, Rita; Baran, Tomasz 2016. Collective Narcissism Predicts Hypersensitivity to In-group Insult and Direct and Indirect Retaliatory Intergroup Hostility. *European Journal of Personality*, 30 (6), 532–551.

Grey Ellis, Emma 2019. Greta Thunberg's Digital Rise Calls Back to a Pre-Digital Era. *Wired* 28.09. www.wired.com/story/greta-thunberg-social-media/.

Griffin, Roger 2002. The Incredible Shrinking Ism: The Survival of Fascism in the Post-fascist Era. *Patterns of Prejudice*, 36 (3), 3–8.

Griffin, Roger 2003. From Slime Mold To Rhizome: An Introduction to the Groupuscular Right. *Patterns of Prejudice*, 37 (1), 27–50.

Grossberg, Lawrence 1992. *We Gotta Get Out of This Place: Popular Conservatism and Postmodern culture*. New York: Routledge.

Grusin, Richard 2010. *Premediation: Affect and Mediality After 9/11*. Basingstoke: Palgrave Macmillan.

Gudkov, Lev 2005. Идеологема врага. In: *Образ врага*, (ed. L. Gudkov). Moscow: O.G.I., 7–79.

Gureeva, Julija; Lužnikova, Anna 2019. Всю ответственность несёт правительство: фонд Сороса призвал Тбилиси бороться с "гибридной войной" РФ против Грузии. *Russia Today* 5.07. https://russian.rt.com/world/article/647256-fond-soros-gruziya-ruso fobiya?fbclid=IwAR20kMN5mbiUMyStUnxgDXdQ1flfN9PavkMllMsCr1waFg0hjjfu FTogTDk.

Hallahan, Kirk; Holtzhausen, Derina; van Ruler, Betteke; Verčič, Dejan; Sriramesh, Krishnamurthy 2007. Defining Strategic Communication. *International Journal of Strategic Communication*, 1 (1), 3–35.

Harsin, Jayson 2014. Public argument in the new media ecology: Implications of temporality, spatiality, and cognition. *Journal of Argumentation in Context*, 3(1), 7–34.

Harsin, Jayson 2015. Regimes of Posttruth, Postpolitics, and Attention Economies. *Communication, Culture & Critique*, 8, 327–333.

Helmus, Todd C.; Bodine-Baron, Elizabeth; Radin, Andrew; Magnuson, Madeline; Mendelsohn, Joshua; Marcellino, William; Bega, Andriy; Winkelman, Zev 2018. *Russian Social Media Influence: Understanding Russian Propaganda in Eastern Europe*. www.rand.org/pubs/research_reports/RR2237.html.

Herman, David 2009. *Basic Elements of Narrative*. Chichester, Malden: Wiley-Blackwell.

Hine, Christine 2015. *Ethnography for the Internet: Embedded, Embodied and Everyday.* London: Bloomsbury Academic.

Hofstadter, Richard 1967. *The Paranoid Style in American Politics and Other Essays.* New York: Vintage Books.

Hopkins, Valerie 2018. Soros-linked University to Move Courses out of Hungary. *Financial Times* 25.10, www.ft.com/content/d1a6074e-d856-11e8-ab8e-6be0dcf18713.

Howard, Robert Glenn 2013. Vernacular Authority: Critically Engaging "Tradition". In: *Tradition in the Twenty-First Century. Locating the Role of the Past in the Present,* (ed. T. Blank; R.G. Howard). Utah: State University Press, 72–99.

Howarth, David; Glynos, Jason 2007. *Logics of Critical Explanation in Social and Political Theory.* Abingdon: Routledge.

Hristov, Todor 2019. *Impossible Knowledge Conspiracy Theories, Power, and Truth.* London, New York: Routledge.

Hume, Tim 2018. How Hungary Helped Make George Soros the Ultimate Villain to Nationalists Around the World. *Vice* 25.11, www.vice.com/en_us/article/yw7pxw/how-hungary-helped-make-george-soros-the-ultimate-villain-to-nationalists-around-the-world.

Hungary: Europe's Champion of Conspiracy Theories. DW interview with Peter Kreko 2018. *Deutsche Welle* 11.12. www.dw.com/en/hungary-europes-champion-of-conspiracy-theories/a-46689822.

Icke, David 1999. *The Biggest Secret: The Book That Will Change the World.* Ryde: Bridge of Love Publications.

Icke, David 2005. *Infinite Love is the Only Truth: Everything Else is Illusion.* Ryde: David Icke Books.

Jakobson, Roman 1971a. Dominant. In: *Readings in Russian Poetics: Formalist and Structuralist Views,* (eds. L. Matejka; K. Pomorska), Cambridge, Mass.: MIT Press, 82–87.

Jakobson, Roman 1971b. Language in Relation to Other Communication Systems. In: *Selected Writings II: Word and Language.* Hague, Paris: Mouton, 697–708.

Jakobson, Roman 1976. Metalanguage as a Linguistic Problem. In: *Selected Writings VII,* The Hague: Mouton, 113–121.

Jantunen, Saara 2018. *Infosõda.* Tallinn: SA Kultuurileht.

Jenkins, Henry 2011. *Transmedia 202: Further Reflections. Confessions of an Aca-Fan: The Official Weblog of Henry Jenkins,* http://henryjenkins.org/2011/08/defining_transmedia_further_re.html.

Johnson, Jessica 2018. The Self-Radicalization of White Men: "Fake News" and the Affective Networking of Paranoia. *Communication Culture & Critique,* 11, 100–115.

Jolley, Daniel; Douglas, Karen M. 2013. The Social Consequences of Conspiracism: Exposure to Conspiracy Theories Decreases Intentions to Engage in Politics and to Reduce One's Carbon Footprint. *British Journal of Psychology,* 105, 35–56.

Jürgen Rooste annab edasi punarohelise maailmavaate kogu tema demagoogias, vihkamises ja võltsmoraalis 2019. *Uued Uudised* 02.08. https://uueduudised.ee/arvamus/juhtkiri/jurgen-rooste-annab-edasi-punarohelise-maailmavaate-kogu-tema-demagoogias-vihkamises-ja-voltsmoraalis/.

Jurgenson, Nathan 2012. When Atoms Meet Bits: Social Media, the Mobile Web and Augmented Revolution. *Future Internet,* 4, 83–91.

Kalmar, Ivan; Stevens, Christopher; Worby, Nicholas 2018. Twitter, Gab, and Racism: The Case of the Soros Myth. *Proceedings of the 9th International Conference on Social Media and Society, Copenhagen* 18–20.07, 330–334.

Karlova, Natascha; Fisher, Karen 2013. "Plz RT": A Social Diffusion Model of Misinformation and Disinformation for Understanding human Information Behaviour. *Proceedings of the ISIC 2012*, 1–17, www.hastac.org/sites/default/files/documents/karlova_12_isic_misdismodel.pdf.

Kasekamp, Andres; Madisson, Mari-Liis; Wierenga, Louis John 2019. Discursive Opportunities for the Estonian Populist Radical Right in a Digital Society. *Problems of Post-Communism*, 1–12.

Kaufman, Michael T. 2002. *Soros: The Life and Times of a Messianic Billionaire*. New York: Knopf.

Keeley, Brian L. 1999. Of Conspiracy Theories. *The Journal of Philosophy*, 3, 109–126.

Kilcullen, David 2013. *Out of the Mountains: The Coming Age of the Urban Guerrilla*. Oxford: Oxford University Press.

Knight, Peter 2002. A Nation of Conspiracy Theorists. In: *Conspiracy Nation: The Politics of Paranoia in Post-War America*, (ed. P. Knight). New York: New York University Press, 1–17.

Knight, Peter 2008. Outrageous Conspiracy Theories: Popular and Official Responses to 9/11 in Germany and The United States. *New German Critique*, 1, 165–195.

Kovács, Attila 2015. The 'New Jihadists' and the Visual Turn from Al-Qa'ida to ISIL/ISIS/Da'ish. *BiztPol Affairs*, 2 (3), 67.

Kragh, Martin; Åsberg, Sebastian 2017. Russia's Strategy for Influence Through Public Diplomacy and Active Measures: The Swedish Case. *Journal of Strategic Studies*, 40 (6), 773–816.

Krasodomski-Jones, Alex 2019. Suspicious Minds: Conspiracy Theories in the Age of Populism. *Demos* 26.04. https://demos.co.uk/project/suspicious-minds-conspiracy-theories-in-the-age-of-populism/.

Krekó, Péter; Enyedi, Zsolt 2018. Orbán's Laboratory of Illiberalism. *Journal of Democracy*, 29 (3), 39–51.

Kress, Gunther 2012. Multimodal Discourse Analysis. In: *The Routledge Handbook of Discourse Analysis* (eds. J.P. Gee; M. Handford). Oxon and New York: Routledge, 35–50.

Kristeva, Julia 1969. *Sémiotiké. Recherches puor une – semianalyse. Essais*. Paris: Le Seuil.

Kui Trump Soros Ekspressi migrandikolonni pidama ei saa, järgnevad sellele miljonid parema elu otsijad 2018. *Uued Uudised* 01.11. https://uueduudised.ee/uudis/maailm/kui-trump-soros-ekspressi-migrandikolonni-pidama-ei-saa-jargnevad-sellele-miljonid-parema-elu-otsijad/.

Laclau, Ernesto 1990. *New Reflections on the Revolution of Our Time*. London and New York: Verso.

Laclau, Ernesto 2005. *On Populist Reason*. London: Verso.

Laclau, Ernesto; Mouffe, Chantal 1985. *Hegemony and Socialist Strategy: Towards a Radical Democratic Politics*. London: Verso.

Larson, Erik V.; Darilek, Richard E.; Gibran, Daniel; Nichiporuk, Brian; Richardson, Amy; Schwartz, Lowell H.; Thurston, Cathryn Q. 2009. *Effective Influence Operations: A Framework for Enhancing Army Capabilities*. Santa Monica, CA: RAND Corporation.

Laver, John 1975. Communicative Functions of Phatic Communion. In: *Organization of Behaviour in Face-to-Face Interaction*, (eds. A. Kendon; R. Harris; M. Key). The Hague: Mouton, 215–238.

Leone, Massimo 2017. Fundamentalism, Anomie, Conspiracy: Umberto Eco's Semiotics against Interpretive Irrationality. In: *Umberto Eco in his Own Words*, (ed. T. Thellefsen). Berlin and Boston: Walter de Gruyter, 221–229.

Leone, Massimo 2019. The Semiotics of the Face in the Digital Era, *Perspectives*, RFIEA.

Leone, Massimo; Madisson, Mari-Liis; Ventsel, Andreas 2020. Semiotic Approaches to Conspiracy Theories. In: *Routledge Handbook of Conspiracy Theories 1st Edition*, (eds. M. Butter; P. Knight). New York: Routledge, 43–54.

Lepik, Peet 2007. *Universals in the Context of Juri Lotman's Semiotics.* Tartu Semiotics Library 7. Tartu: Tartu University Press.

Lewandowsky, Stephan; Ecker, Ullrich K.H; Cook, John 2017. Beyond Misinformation: Understanding and Coping with the "Post-Truth" Era. *Journal of Applied Research in Memory and Cognition*, 6 (4), 353–369.

Lewandowsky, Stephan; Gignac, Gilles E.; Oberauer, Klaus 2013. The Role of Conspiracist Ideation and Worldviews in Predicting Rejection of Science. *PLOS ONE*, 10 (8), 1–12.

Liu, James H.; Hilton, Denis J. 2010. How the Past Weighs on the Present: Social Representation of History and Their Role in Identity Politics. *British Journal of Social Psychology*, 44 (4), 537–556.

Livingston, Steven; Nassetta, Jack 2018. Framing and Strategic Narratives: Synthesis and Analytical Framework. *SAIS Review of International Affairs*, 38 (2), 101–110.

Lotman, Juri 1982. The Text and the Structure of Its Audience. *New Literary History*, 14 (1), 81–87.

Lotman, Juri 1988a. The Semiotics of Culture and the Concept of Text. *Soviet Psychology*, 26 (3), 52–58.

Lotman, Juri 1988b. Text Within a Text. *Soviet Psychology*, 26 (3), 32–51.

Lotman, Juri 1997. Culture as a Subject and an Object in Itself. *Trames* 1 (51/46), 7–16.

Lotman, Juri 2000. *Universe of the Mind: A Semiotic Theory of Culture.* Bloomington and Indianapolis: Indiana University Press.

Lotman, Juri 2005. On Semiosphere. *Sign Systems Studies*, 33 (1), 205–229.

Lotman, Juri 2006. Kirjandus ja mütoloogia. In: *Kultuurisemiootika*, Tallinn: Olion, 273–298.

Lotman, Juri 2007. *Hirm ja segadus: Esseid kultuurisemiootikast*, (ed. M. Lotman). Tallinn: Varrak.

Lotman, Juri 2010. *Kultuuritüpoloogiad.* Tartu: Tartu Ülikooli Kirjastus.

Lotman, Juri 2019. The Symbol in the System of Culture. In: *Culture, Memory and History*, (ed. M. Tamm). Cham: Palgrave Macmillan, 161–173.

Lotman, Juri; Uspenskij, Boris 1975. Myth-name-Culture. *Soviet Studies in Literature: A Journal of Translations*, 11 (2/3), 17–46.

Lotman, Juri; Uspenskij, Boris 1978. On the Semiotic Mechanism of Culture. *New Literary History*, 9 (2), 211–232.

Lotman, Juri; Uspenskij, Boris 1984. The Role of Dual Models in the Dynamics of Russian Culture (Up to the End of the Eighteenth Century). In: *The Semiotics of Russian Culture*, (ed. A. Shukman). Ann Arbor: University of Michigan Press, 3–28.

Lotman, Juri; Ivanov, Vjacheslav; Toporov, Vladimir; Pjatigorskij, Aleksander; Uspenskij, Boris 2013. Theses on the Semiotic Study of Cultures (as Applied to the Slavic texts). In: *Beginnings of the Semiotics of Culture*, (eds. S. Salupere; P. Torop; K. Kull). *Tartu Semiotics Library 13*, Tartu: Tartu University Press, 51–77.

Lotman, Mihhail 2007. Hirm ja segadus – irratsionaalse semioosi poole. In: J. Lotman. *Hirm ja segadus. Esseid kultuurisemiootikast*, (ed. M. Lotman). Tallinn: Varrak, 141–158.

Madisson, Mari-Liis 2014. The Semiotic Logic of Signification of Conspiracy Theories. *Semiotica*, 202, 273–300.

Madisson, Mari-Liis 2016a. *The Semiotic Construction of Identities in Hypermedia Environments: The Analysis of Online Communication of the Estonian Extreme Right.* Tartu: Tartu University Press.

Madisson, Mari-Liis 2016b. NWO Conspiracy Theory: A Key Frame in Online Communication of Estonian Extreme Right. *Lexia*, 23/24, 189–208.

Madisson, Mari-Liis; Ventsel, Andreas 2016a. Autocommunicative Meaning-making in Online Communication of Estonian Extreme Right. *Sign Systems Studies*, 44 (3), 326–354.

Madisson, Mari-Liis; Ventsel, Andreas 2016b. "Freedom of Speech" in the Self-Descriptions of the Estonian Extreme Right Groupuscules. *National Identities*, 18 (2), 89–104.

Madisson, Mari-Liis; Ventsel, Andreas 2018. Groupuscular Identity-creation in Online Communication of Estonian Extreme Right. *Semiotica*, 222, 25–46.

Madisson, Tiit 2018. Juudi "revolutsionäärid" maailma ümber kujundamas. *Blog Rahvuslane* http://rahvuslane.blogspot.com/2018/05/juudi-revolutsionaarid-maailma-umber.html.

Majakovski, Vladimir 2013. *Selected Poems*, (trans. J. H. McGavran III). Evanston: Northwestern University Press.

Maksimov, Aldo 2019. Repliik: Tallinna Ülikool – propagandaasutus või ülikool? *Objektiiv* 08.07. https://objektiiv.ee/repliik-tallinna-ulikool-propagandaasutus-voi-ulikool/.

Marchart, Oliver 2007. *Post-Foundational Political Thought: Political Difference in Nancy, Lefort, Badiou and Laclau.* Edinburgh: Edinburgh University Press.

Marmura, Stephen M.E. 2014. Likely and Unlikely Stories: Conspiracy Theories in an Age of Propaganda. *International Journal of Communication*, 8, 2377–2395.

Marwick, Alice; Lewis, Rebecca 2017. *Media Manipulation and Disinformation Online.* https://datasociety.net/output/media-manipulation-and-disinfo-online/.

McLaughlin, Neil; Trilupaityte, Skaidra 2012. The International Circulation of Attacks and the Reputational Consequences of Local Context: George Soros's Difficult Reputation in Russia, Post-Soviet Lithuania and the United States. *Cultural Sociology*, 7 (4), 431–446.

Melley, Timothy 2002. *Empire of Conspiracy: The Culture of Paranoia in Postwar America.* New York: Cornell University Press.

Mesežnikov, Grigorij 2019. The EU, Russia, Ukraine in Slovak Pro-Russian Media. http://4liberty.eu/the-eu-russia-ukraine-in-slovak-pro-russian-media/.

Miller, Vincent 2008. New Media, Networking and Phatic Culture. *Convergence*, 14, 387–400.

Miskimmon, Alister; O'Loughlin, Ben 2019. Narratives of the EU in Israel/Palestine: Narrative "stickiness" and the Formation of Expectations. *European Security*, 28 (3), 268–283.

Miskimmon, Alister; O'Loughlin, Ben; Roselle, Laura 2013. *Strategic Narratives, Communication Power and the New World Order.* New York: Routledge.

Miskimmon, Alister; O'Loughlin, Ben; Roselle, Laura 2017. Introduction. In: *Forging the World: Strategic Narratives and International Relations*, (eds. A. Miskimmon; B. O'Loughlin; L. Roselle). Ann Arbor: University of Michigan Press, 1–22.

Monaci, Sara 2017. Explaining the Islamic State's Online Media Strategy: A Transmedia Approach. *International Journal of Communication*, 11, 2842–2860.

Mouffe, Chantal 2005. *On the Political.* London, New York: Routledge.

Murphy, Margi 2018. YouTube to Fight Conspiracy Theory Videos by Showing Users Wikipedia Links. *The Telegraph* 09.07. www.telegraph.co.uk/technology/2018/07/09/youtube-fight-conspiracy-theory-videos-showing-users-wikipedia/.

Murray, Janet H. 1997. *Hamlet on the Holodeck: The Future of Narrative in Cyberspace.* New York: The Free Press.

Nazaryan, Alexander 2017. No, Trump Supporters, the San Francisco Chronicle didn't Prove your Point about 'Paid' Protesters. *Newsweek* 08.05. www.newsweek.com/ trump-paid-protesters-san-francisco-chronicle-alt-right-596511.

Nissen, Thomas Elkjær 2015. *The Weaponization of Social Media: Characteristics of Contemporary Conflicts.* Copenhagen: Royal Danish Defence College.

Novak, Benjamin 2017. Satan is Using the Soros Plan and Brussels to Usher in the Apocalypse! *Budapest Beacon* 09.10. https://budapestbeacon.com/satan-using-soros-plan-brussels-usher-apocalypse/.

O'Halloran, Kay L.; Marissa K.L.E.; Podlasov, Alexey; Tan, Sabine 2013. Multimodal Digital Semiotics: The Interaction of Language with Other Resources. *Text & Talk*, 33 (4/5), 665–690.

Ojamaa, Maarja 2015. *The Transmedial Aspect of Cultural Autocommunication.* Tartu: Tartu University Press.

Ojamaa, Maarja; Torop, Peeter 2015. Transmediality of Cultural Autocommunication. *International Journal of Cultural Studies*, 18 (1), 61–78.

O'Loughlin, Ben; Miskimmon, Alister; Roselle, Laura 2017. Strategic Narratives: Methods and Ethics. In: *Forging the World: Strategic Narratives and International Relations*, (eds. A. Miskimmon; B. O'Loughlin; L. Roselle). Ann Arbor: University of Michigan Press. 23–55.

Önnerfors, Andreas 2019. "The Great Replacement" – Decoding the Christchurch Terrorist Manifesto. www.radicalrightanalysis.com/2019/03/18/the-great-replacement-decoding-the-christchurch-terrorist-manifesto/.

Papacharissi, Zizi 2014. *Affective Publics. Sentiment, Technology, and Politics.* New York: Oxford University Press.

Papacharissi, Zizi 2016. Affective Publics and Structures of Storytelling: Sentiment, Events and Mediality. *Information, Communication & Society*, 19 (3), 307–324.

Papernyi, Vladimir 1996. *Культура "Два".* Moscow: NLO Press.

Peirce, Charles Sanders 1932. *Collected Papers of Charles Sanders Peirce.* Harvard: Harvard University Press.

Perlmutter, David D. 1998. *Photojournalism and Foreign Policy: Icons of Outrage in International Crises.* Westport, CT: Greenwood.

Peterson, Bo 2013. Mirror, Mirror … Myth-making, Self-images and the View of the US "Other" in Contemporary Russia. In: *Russia's Identity in International Relations: Images, Perceptions, Misperceptions*, (ed. R. Taras). London: Routledge, 11–23.

Phillips DeZalia, Rebekah A.; Moeschberger, Scott L. 2014. The Function of Symbols that Bind and Divide. In: *Symbols that Bind, Symbols that Divide the Semiotics of Peace and Conflict*, (ed. S.L. Moeschberger; R.A. Phillips DeZalia). New York: Springer, 1–12.

Piata, Anna 2016. When Metaphor Becomes a Joke: Metaphor Journeys from Political Ads to Internet Memes. *Journal of Pragmatics*, 106, 39–56.

Pipes, Daniel 1999. *Conspiracy: How the Paranoid Style Flourishes and Where It Comes From.* New York: The Free Press.

Pomerantsev, Peter; Weiss, Michael 2014. *The Menace of Unreality: How the Kremlin Weaponizes Information, Culture and Money.* New York: Institute of Modern Russia, www.stratcomcoe.org/peter-pomerantsev-michael-weiss-menace-unreality-how-kremlin-weaponizes-information-culture-and.

Poola proovib peatada Sorost soetamast suurt raadiojaama 2019. *Objektiiv* 27.01. https:// objektiiv.ee/poola-proovib-peatada-sorost-soetamast-suurt-raadiojaama/.

President Donald Trump süüdistas maailmalammutajat George Sorosit laimukampaania rahastamises 2018. *Uued Uudised* 05.10. https://uueduudised.ee/uudis/maailm/president-donald-trump-suudistas-maailmalammutajat-george-sorosit-laimukampaania-rahastamises/.

Prøitz, Lin 2017. Visual Social Media and Affectivity: The Impact of the Image of Aylan Kurdi and Young People's Response to the Refugee Crisis in Oslo and Sheffield. *Information, Communication & Society*, 1–16.

"Räägime asjast": kõigieestlastest, Kaja Kallasest, koalitsioonist ja rahastamisest 2019. *Uued Uudised* 14.04. https://uueduudised.ee/uudis/eesti/raagime-asjast-koigieestlastest-kaja-kallasest-koalitsioonist-ja-rahastamisest/.

Radovanovic, Danica; Ragnedda, Massimo 2012. Small Talk in the Digital Age: Making Sense of Phatic Posts. *#MSM2012 2nd Workshop on Making Sense of Microposts*, 10–13.

Radžvilas, Vytautas 2008. Už pilietiškumo miražų – "pilietinė" nomenklatūra. www.balsas.lt/naujiena/183154/vytautas-radzvilas-uz-pilietiskumo-mirazu-pilietine-nomenklatura/1.

Rahvusriikide lammutaja Soros sekkub Eesti valimistesse – Raul Rebane tõestas seda 2019. *Uued Uudised* 05.01. https://uueduudised.ee/uudis/eesti/rahvusriikide-lammutaja-soros-sekkub-eesti-valimistesse-raul-rebane-toestas-seda/.

Rahvusriike vaenav vanurist miljardär George Soros üritab oma rahaga Brexitit peatada 2018. *Uued Uudised* 02.08. https://uueduudised.ee/uudis/maailm/rahvusriike-vaenav-vanurist-miljardar-george-soros-uritab-oma-rahaga-brexitit-peatada/.

Rändekriis Vahemerel — kas vaid Liibüa rannavalve töötab selle nimel, et migrandid mere lõunakaldale jääks? 2018. *Uued Uudised* 22.06. https://uueduudised.ee/uudis/maailm/randekriis-vahemerel-kas-vaid-liibua-rannavalve-tootab-selle-nimel-et-migrandid-mere-lounakaldale-jaaks/.

Rebane, Raul 2018. 10 levinumat vandenõuteooriat Venemaal. *ERR* 27.08. www.err.ee/856514/raul-rebane-10-levinumat-vandenouteooriat-venemaal.

Ringsmose, Jens; Børgesen, Berit K. 2011. Shaping Public Attitudes Towards the Deployment of Military Power: NATO, Afghanistan and the Use of Strategic Narratives. *European Security*, 20 (4), 505–528.

Robertson, Pat 1991. *The New World Order*. Nashville: Word Records.

Roselle, Laura, Miskimmon, Alister; O'Loughlin, Ben 2014. Strategic Narrative: A New Means to Understand Soft Power. *Media, War and Conflict*, 7 (1), 70–84.

Saavik, Siim 2017. *Eesti alternatiivmeedia kanalite Nihilist, Vanglaplaneet ja Uued Uudised toimimine ning funktsioonid*. Tartu Ülikool, Ühiskonnateaduste instituut. Bakalaureusetöö.

Saldre, Maarja; Torop, Peeter 2012. Transmedia Space. In: *Crossmedia Innovations: Texts, Markets, Institutions*, (eds. I. Ibrus; C. Scolari). Frankfurt am Main: Peter Lang Publishers House, 25–44.

Salvatore, Sergio; Freda, Maria 2011. Affect, Unconscious and Sensemaking. A Psychodynamic, Semiotic and Dialogic Model. *New Ideas in Psychology*, 29 (2), 119–135.

Saussure, de Ferdinand 2011. *Course in General Linguistics*. New York: Columbia University Press.

Schöpflin, George 2010. The Dilemmas of Identity. Tallinn: Tallinn University Press.

Schrich, Lisa 2005. *Ritual and Symbol in Peacebuilding*. Bloomfield, CT: Kumarian Press.

Schwartau, Winn 1996. *Information Warfare: Chaos on the Information Superhighway*. New York, NY: Thunder's Mouth Press.

Selg, Peeter; Ventsel, Andreas 2008. Towards a Semiotic Theory of Hegemony: Naming as Hegemonic Operation in Lotman and Laclau. *Sign Systems Studies*, 36 (1), 167–183.

Selg, Peeter; Ventsel, Andreas 2010. An Outline for a Semiotic Theory of Hegemony. *Semiotica*, 182, 443–474.

Selg, Peeter; Ventsel, Andreas 2020. *Introducing Relational Political Analysis: Political Semiotics as a Theory and Method.* Palgrave (forthcoming).

Skandaalne Soros toetab oma rahadega sisserännet Itaaliasse ja sealt edasi kogu Euroopasse 2019. *Uued Uudised* 28.10. https://uueduudised.ee/uudis/maailm/skandaalne-soros-toetab-oma-rahadega-sisserannet-itaaliasse-ja-sealt-edasi-kogu-euroopasse/.

Siibak, Andra 2012. Being Publicly Private: Extreme Nationalist User Practices on Social Networks. In: *Security in Cyberspace: Targeting Nations, Infrastructures, Individuals*, (ed. G. Giamello). London and New York: Bloomsbury, 215–230.

Silverman, Craig 2015. *Lies, Damn Lies, and Viral Content.* Columbia Journalism School, http://towcenter.org/wp-content/uploads/2015/02/LiesDamnLies_Silverman_TowCenter.pdf.

Singer, Peter Warren; Brooking, Emerson T. 2018. *LikeWar: The Weaponization of Social Media.* Boston, New York: Eamon Dolan/Houghton Mifflin Harcourt.

Soros saalib Brüsseli vahet, et Orbánile karistust kaubelda 2018. *Objektiiv* 23.04. https://objektiiv.ee/soros-saalib-brusseli-vahet-et-orbanile-karistust-kaubelda/.

Sorose rahastavad propagandaasutused hakkavad Ungari tolmu jalgadelt pühkima 2018. *Uued Uudised* 21.04. https://uueduudised.ee/uudis/maailm/sorose-rahastavad-propagandaasutused-hakkavad-ungari-tolmu-jalgadelt-puhkima/.

Soukup, Charles 2008. 9/11 Conspiracy Theories on the World Wide Web: Digital Rhetoric and Alternative Epistemology. *Journal of Literacy and Technology*, 9 (3), 2–25.

Stæhr, Andreas 2014. The Appropriation of Transcultural Flows Among Copenhagen Youth – The Case of Illuminati. *Discourse, Context & Media*, 4/5, 101–115.

Stano, Simona 2020. The Internet and the Spread of Conspiracy Content. In: *Routledge Handbook of Conspiracy Theories 1st Edition*, (eds. M. Butter; P. Knight). New York: Routledge, 438–496.

Statello, Clara 2019. Oliver Stone a Taormina per presentare Revealing Ukraine in prima visione mondiale. *Sputnik* 05.07. https://it.sputniknews.com/opinioni/201907057848087-oliver-stone-a-taormina-per-presentare-revealing-ukraine-in-prima-visione-mondiale/.

Sunstein, Cas; Vermeule, Adrian 2009. Conspiracy Theories: Causes and Cures. *Journal of Political Philosophy*, 17 (2), 202–227.

Swimelar, Safia 2018. Deploying Images of Enemy Bodies: US Image Warfare and Strategic Narratives. *Media, War and Conflict*, 11 (2), 179–203.

Tan, Sabine; O'Halloran, Kay L.; Wignell, Peter; Chai, Kevin; Lange, Rebecca 2018. A Multimodal Mixed Methods Approach for Examining Recontextualisation Patterns of Violent Extremist Images in Online Media. *Discourse, Context and Media*, 21, 18–35.

Tiidenberg, Katrin 2017. *Ihu ja hingega internetis.* Tallinn: Tallinn University Press.

Tiidenberg, Katrin; Siibak, Andra 2018. Affordances, Affect and Audiences – Making Sense of Networked Publics, Introduction to AoIR 2017 Special Issue on Networked Publics. *Studies in transition states and societies*, 10 (2), 1–9.

Todorov, Tzvetan 1977. *Theories du Symbole.* Paris: Ed. Seuil.

Tõnisson, Roland 2018. Messias Soros. Mõtteid globalismist. *Objektiiv* 15.03. https://objektiiv.ee/messias-soros-motteid-globalismist/.

Tõnisson, Roland 2019. Poliitkorrektsus on vasakliberaalide võimuhaaramise vahend. *Uued Uudised* 11.08. https://uueduudised.ee/arvamus/roland-tonisson-poliitkorrektsus-on-vasakradikaalide-voimuhaaramise-vahend/.

Trump tuleb: multikultilased, soroslased, sallivuslased ja muud friigid, värisege! 2017. *Uued Uudised* 21.01. https://uueduudised.ee/arvamus/juhtkiri/trump-tuleb-multikultilased-soroslased-sallivuslased-ja-muud-friigid-varisege/.

Trumpi tagandamiskatse taga on Sorosi propagandatööstus 2019. *Objektiiv* 27.09. https:// objektiiv.ee/trumpi-tagandamiskatse-taga-on-sorose-propagandatoostus/.

Tufekci, Zeynep 2013. "Not This One": Social Movements, the Attention Economy, and Microcelebrity Networked Activism. *American Behavioral Scientist*, 57 (7), 848–870.

Turner-Graham, Emily 2014. "Breivik is my Hero": The Dystopian World of Extreme Right Youth on the Internet. *Australian Journal of Politics and History*, 60 (3), 416–430.

Ühe majanduspõgenikust aafriklase juhtum: "Hüvasti Itaalia, sa valmistasid mulle suure pettumuse!" 2018. *Uued Uudised* 25.07. https://uueduudised.ee/uudis/maailm/uhe-majanduspogenikust-aafriklase-juhtum-huvasti-itaalia-sa-valmistasid-mulle-suure-pettumuse.

Ungari annab seadustepaketiga "Stop Soros" valusa hoobi illegaalse immigratsiooni käsilastele 2018. *Uued Uudised* 04.06. https://uueduudised.ee/uudis/maailm/ungari-annab-seadustepaketiga-stop-sorosvalusa-hoobi-illegaalse-immigratsiooni-kasilastele/.

Ungari hoiatab "Sorose ekspressi" eest Ameerikas ja Euroopas 2018. *Objektiiv* 30.10 https://objektiiv.ee/ungari-hoiatab-sorose-ekspressi-eest-ameerikas-ja-euroopas/.

Ungari valitsus: laupäevase meeleavalduse korraldas Soros 2018. *Objektiiv* 17.04. https:// objektiiv.ee/ungari-valitsus-laupaevase-meeleavalduse-korraldas-soros/.

Ungaris toimub Sorose asjus suur rahvaküsitlus 2017. *Objektiiv* 15.09. https://objektiiv. ee/ungaris-toimub-sorose-asjus-suur-rahvakusitlus/.

Uscinski, Joseph E.; Parent, Joseph M. 2014. *American Conspiracy Theories*. New York, NY: Oxford University Press.

Uspenskij, Boris 2013. Moskva-Tartu kultuurisemiootika koolkonnast. In: *Vene kultuuri jõujooni. Valik artikleid*. Tartu: Ilmamaa, 20–23.

Vaher, Martin 2019. Feministide välimääraja: kes on Eesti naiste eest marssijad? *Objektiiv* 31.01. https://objektiiv.ee/feministide-valimaaraja-kes-eesti-naiste-eest-marssijad/.

Valitsus: Ungari valimistesse on sekkunud tuhanded soroslased 2018. *Objektiiv* 27.03. https://objektiiv.ee/valitsus-ungari-valimistesse-sekkunud-tuhanded-soroslased/.

Valsiner, Jaan 2007. *Culture in Minds and Societies: Foundations of Cultural Psychology*. New Delhi: Sage.

van Dijck, Jose 2013. *The Culture of Connectivity: A Critical History of Social Media*. New York: Oxford University Press.

van Dijk, Teun 1998. *Ideology. A Multidisciplinary Approach*. London: Sage.

van Niekerk, Brett; Maharaj, Manoj 2013. Social Media and Information Conflict. *International Journal of Communication*, 7, 1162–1184.

van Prooijen, Jan-Willem; Douglas, Karen M. 2018. Belief in Conspiracy Theories: Basic Principles of an Emerging Research Domain. *European Journal of Social Psychology*, 1–12.

Vatikani diil globalistide ja soroslastega: pedofiilia mahavaikimise eest geiagenda ja multikultijutt 2018. *Uued Uudised* 25.09, https://uueduudised.ee/uudis/maailm/ vatikani-diil-globalistide-ja-soroslastega-pedofiilia-mahavaikimise-eest-geiagenda-ja-multikultijutt/.

Ventsel, Andreas 2007. The Construction of the We-category: Political Rhetoric in Soviet Estonia from June 1940 to July 1941. *Sign Systems Studies*, 35, 249–267.

Ventsel, Andreas 2009a. *Towards Semiotic Theory of Hegemony*. Tartu: Tartu University Press.

Ventsel, Andreas 2009b. The Role of Political Rhetoric in the Development of Soviet Totalitarian Language. *Russian Journal of Communication*, 2, 9–26.

Ventsel, Andreas 2011. Hegemonic Signification from Cultural Semiotics Point of View. *Sign Systems Studies*, 39 (2/4), 58–88.

Ventsel, Andreas 2014. Hegemonic Signification from Perspective of Visual Rhetoric. *Semiotica*, 199, 175–192.

Ventsel, Andreas 2016a. Political Potentiality of Conspiracy Theories. *Lexia*, 23/24, 309–326.

Ventsel, Andreas 2016b. Rhetorical Transformation in Estonian Political Discourse During World War II. *Semiotica*, 208, 103–132.

Ventsel, Andreas; Madisson, Mari-Liis 2017. Tõejärgne diskursus ja semiootika. *Acta Semiotica Estica*, XIV, 93–116.

Ventsel, Andreas; Hansson, Sten; Madisson, Mari-Liis; Sazonov, Vladimir 2019. Discourse of Fear in Strategic Narratives: The Case of Russia's Zapad War Games. *Media, War & Conflict*, 1–19.

Vincent, Cédric 2006. Mapping the Invisible: Notes on the Reason of Conspiracy Theories. In: *Sarai Reader*, (eds. M. Narula; S. Sengupta; R. Sundaram; J. Bagchi; A. Sharan; G. Lovink). Delhi: Centre for the Study of Developing Societies, 41–48.

Vogel, Kenneth P.; Shane, Scott; Kingsley, Patrick 2018. How Vilification of George Soros Moved from the Fringes to the Mainstream. *The New York Times* 31.10. www.nytimes.com/2018/10/31/us/politics/george-soros-bombs-trump.html.

von Stackelberg, Peter; Jones, Ruth 2014. Tales of Our Tomorrows: Transmedia Storytelling and Communicating about the Future. *Journal of Futures Studies* 18 (3), 57–76.

Walker, Shaun 2018. University Founded by George Soros "forced out" of Hungary. *The Guardian* 25.10. www.theguardian.com/world/2018/oct/25/university-founded-by-george-soros-forced-out-of-hungary.

Weaver, Courtney; Hopkins, Valerie 2018.The Soros Conspiracy Theory goes Global. *Financial Times* 04.11. www.ft.com/content/e2a1ecb0-dc0d-11e8-9f04-38d397e6661c.

Weimann, David 2003. Internet. In: *Conspiracy Theories in American History: An Encyclopedia*, (ed. P. Knight), Santa Barbara, Denver, Oxford: ABC CLIO, 347–349.

Wetoszka, Adam 2016. An Attempt to Identify Hybrid Conflict. *Sõjateadlane* (Estonian Journal of Military Studies), 54–66.

White, Hayden 2003. Kirjandusteooria jab ajalookirjutus. *Tuna*, 1, 111–127.

Wiggins, Bradley E. 2017. Navigating an Immersive Narratology: Factors to Explain the Reception of Fake News. *International Journal of E-Politics*, 13, 16–29.

Williams, David 2018. Denver's Airport Pokes Fun at Conspiracy Theories. Walls are Hiding Construction, Not Lizard People. *CNN Travel* 07.09. https://edition.cnn.com/travel/article/denver-dia-airport-conspiracy-trnd/index.html.

Willman, Skip 2000. Spinning Paranoia: The Ideologies of Conspiracy and Contingency in Postmodern Culture. In: *Conspiracy Nation: The Politics of Paranoia in Post War America*, (ed. P. Knight). New York: New York University Press, 21–39.

Wisnicki, Adrian 2007. *Conspiracy, Revolution, and Terrorism from Victorian Fiction to the Modern Novel*. New York: Routledge.

Wodak, Ruth 2015. *The Politics of Fear: What Right-Wing Populist Discourses Mean*. London: Sage.

Wolfson, Sam 2018. "Remodelling the Lizard People's Lair": Denver Airport Trolls Conspiracy Theorists. *The Guardian* 07.09. www.theguardian.com/us-news/2018/sep/07/denver-airport-construction-conspiracy-lizard-people.

Wong, Julia Carrie 2018a. Twitter Permanently Bans Conspiracy Theorist Alex Jones. *The Guardian* 06.09. www.theguardian.com/technology/2018/sep/06/twitter-permanently-bans-conspiracy-theorist-alex-jones.

Wong, Julia Carrie 2018b. Facebook Policy Chief Admits Hiring PR Firm to Attack George Soros. *The Guardian* 22.11. www.theguardian.com/technology/2018/nov/21/facebook-admits-definers-pr-george-soros-critics-sandberg-zuckerberg.

Wong, Julia Carrie 2018c. Zuckerberg: I Didn't Know of Facebook Ties to Firm that Attacked George Soros. *The Guardian* 15.11. www.theguardian.com/technology/2018/nov/15/mark-zuckerberg-facebook-george-soros-antisemitism.

Yablokov, Ilja 2015. Conspiracy Theories as a Russian Public Diplomacy Tool: The Case of Russia Today (RT). *Politics*, 35 (3/4), 301–315.

Yablokov, Ilja 2018. *Fortress Russia: Conspiracy Theories in the Post-Soviet World*. Cambridge: Polity.

Zhabotynska, Svetlana; Velivchenko, Valentina 2019. New Media and Strategic Narratives: The Dutch Referendum on Ukraine – EU Association Agreement in Ukrainian and Russian Internet Blogs. *European Security*, 28 (3), 360–381.

Index